T0067190

Change 1 Behavior

IMPROVE YOUR LIFE

SHARON W. PENN

BALBOA. PRESS

A DIVISION OF HAY HOUSE

Balboa Press books may be ordered through booksellers or by contacting:

Balboa Press
A Division of Hay House
1663 Liberty Drive
Bloomington, IN 47403
www.balboapress.com
1 (877) 407-4847

Because of the dynamic nature of the Internet, any web addresses or links contained in
this book may have changed since publication and may no longer be valid. The views
expressed in this work are solely those of the author and do not necessarily reflect the
views of the publisher, and the publisher hereby disclaims any responsibility for them.

The author of this book does not dispense medical advice or prescribe the use of any
technique as a form of treatment for physical, emotional, or medical problems without the
advice of a physician, either directly or indirectly. The intent of the author is only to offer
information of a general nature to help you in your quest for emotional and spiritual well-
being. In the event you use any of the information in this book for yourself, which is your
constitutional right, the author and the publisher assume no responsibility for your actions.

Any people depicted in stock imagery provided by Thinkstock are models,
and such images are being used for illustrative purposes only.
Certain stock imagery © Thinkstock.

Print information available on the last page.

ISBN: 978-1-5043-7188-9 (sc)
ISBN: 978-1-5043-7189-6 (e)

Balboa Press rev. date: 07/11/2017

Dedication

This book is dedicated to
my children and grandchildren.

I especially want to thank my daughters,
<u>Jane Hinton</u> and <u>Diane Jeffers</u>,
who have been a tremendous help with this book.
It's been more fun to write it with their help
of ideas, feedback, editing, and total support.

Acknowledgements

I would not have been able to write this book without the help of the research groups and individuals who were willing to test the concepts of changing behaviors. Making the changes would not have been easy if we had not had each other for the tasks. Thanks to each of you in the name of friendship and science.

I want to thank the many friends who helped me by reading and commenting on the chapters, and those who encouraged me to write.

Emily C. Winslett is my good friend from kindergarten days. We named our daughters for each other, traveled to Europe together, and have remained friends all these years. I thought of her often as I was writing the chapter on friendship, and she helped me with the chapter on spirituality.

Ellen Waldrop, my sister-in-law and good friend, who is the greatest cheerleader to me, and was a wonderful wife to my brother, Rick. I'm so glad that he found her and had many good years with her before his death.

Margaret Click, Ph.D., Marge was a participant and consultant in my first research project on behavioral change for this book. We also worked together as psychotherapists in private practice. She brings much honesty, knowledge, insight, joy, and enthusiasm to any task, and I consider it a privilege to have her as a friend.

And, I want to acknowledge my late husband, Donald Pennington. He was my rock and my inspiration, always praising my writings, and was my unconditional supporter who helped me complete college with a master's degree in social work while we were raising our children. He showed me what trustworthiness was in a relationship.

Relationships

This book about change is focused on how people relate to each other. Our relationships with God, other people, and ourselves are the cornerstones of our lives.

One of those relationships is about my two daughters who are depicted on the front of the book. They are seen here, on this page, in an early shot when they were babies.

Following are notes Jane recently wrote to Diane that demonstrate the importance of their connection. Diane has come to the aid of each family member in many ways over the years, and she continues to do so. She is a kind and compassionate person with unconditional love for all of us. We would do well to take lessons from her.

Jane recently put her life on hold and came to help Diane during and after surgery. I wish for you an important relationship such as this:

"Happy birthday wishes to my sister and best friend! You've always been there for me when I needed you! Hope today and the next year bring you every good thing you deserve!! I love you!!!!"

Another on Sibling's Day in April: "I have the best sister anyone could ask for, and I'm so happy she's mine. Love you bunches and thanks for all you do."

Contents

IF YOU ARE LOOKING IN THIS BOOK FOR HELP:

~Physical Health:

~Mental Health:

~Relationships:

Introduction

A GUIDE FOR LIFE

"To exist is to change, To change is to mature,
To mature is to go on creating oneself endlessly."
Henri Bergson

This book about change is a guide you can use for the rest of your life. It can be like the friend you look to in times of need, or it can be used as an aid when someone you know is requesting your help. Open it to any chapter and you will see hope, a way to change behavior patterns slowly, and a way of life.

You can get to know this new friend in several ways. Begin by checking out the chapter titles on the Contents Page. The first three chapters prepare you to know that people can change and have a better life, and, if needed, where to go for more help. Chapters 4 – 14 have different behaviors to consider. You'll see behaviors that many people want to enhance a bit, or even change. Maybe you'll only want to tweak one or two things.

You begin by working to change one behavior at a time, and you will see how great you feel and how positively people respond to you. You may incorporate those changes into your life and then wait a while to try other behavior changes. You will do best when you move at your own pace—one week, one month, or longer on each behavior. Some people believe it takes more than 30 days to change a behavior and make it a habit; other opinions range from 21 days to 66 days. You'll know when your habit has become automatic. Please inform me when your behavior change becomes a habit and how long it took. *Email me: sharonwpenn@gmail.com*

This book is not meant to replace the need for mental health counseling. If you or someone you know needs professional help, please contact a mental health provider or call your family doctor. Please see the Chapter Notes for more information. (See the Contents for Chapter Notes page number.)

Research teams and individuals working with me tested the behaviors and tasks that are used in this book to make sure they are both workable and changeable. Mental health professional consultants were available at all times and were a part of the research teams that met often. The groups stayed in touch with me and each other by email and telephone, sometimes on a daily basis.

There are 11 chapters on behavior changes (Chapters 4 - 14) in this book—one for each behavior goal addressed. (Please see the Contents page.) You probably will not work on every goal listed in the book. You will have priorities at this time, and later you may have other behaviors you will choose to enhance or change. Each chapter is arranged so that if you decide to work on a particular behavior, you can start there and not have to read guidelines in another area of the book.

Each chapter is self-contained, which makes it user-friendly. There are assessments at the end of each chapter on most behaviors addressed for you to complete (also located in the Worksheet Section). The worksheet number corresponds to the chapter number. When there are two assessments to a chapter, they are labeled *A and B*.

I've created posters for the behaviors covered in the book. They are included in both the behavior chapter contents and a Posters Section. You can print these to display as a reminder that you are making a change and have the guidelines posted.

The behaviors addressed in this book:
~Aging (attitude, memory, pain)
~Anger
~Approachability

~Depression (blues busters)
~Friendships
~Happiness
~Healthy Living (diet, exercise, sleep)
~Humor and Fun
~Relationships for Couples
~Self-Esteem
~Spirituality

Additional behaviors will be addressed on my website: www. *sharonwpenn.com*. Some of the behaviors discussed later will be:

~Communicate Clearly
~Conflict Resolution and Cooperation
~Forgiveness
~Gratitude and Generosity
~Memory and Alzheimer's Disease
~Mindfulness for Self-Awareness
~Motivation, Tolerance, and Patience
~Positive Thoughts & Expressions
~Reasoning with Unreasonable People
~Stress Points & Self-Soothing

Please tell me the behaviors you'd like to see addressed first, suggestions for additional behavior-change information you may want, and your comments on this book's usefulness. Email me: *sharonwpenn@ gmail.com*

Complete the Checklist and Sign a Contract. You will find, at the end of each behavior chapter (4 – 14), a checklist and contract which, if you decide to make a behavior change, you can make a copy, sign it, and place it where you will see it often. The checking off of the commitments you will make and the signing of the contract will *reinforce* that you are committed to the goal of changing or improving that particular behavior, and have agreed to make the changes addressed in that chapter. Review the contract often to keep focused on your goal.

Groups Change Together. You may want to get together with other like-minded people using this book to bring about change. My research has shown that by supporting one another, we can stick to something longer and more consistently. Our research teams found this to be true. We met together regularly to discuss how the tasks were useful, what worked for them and what did not, and we became closer because we had shared goals. This group effort was a motivator which encouraged people to stick with the program. Try it; you will see that it works. Just two people working on a common goal can be the key to success.

Keep a Journal. You may want to keep a journal about your progress and your feelings as you work toward behavior changes. Writing something down in a journal helps in at least two ways. It can be used as a "road map" to help you see where you have been and where you are going. It can also be a record of validity—reminding you that you are making changes and how it is occurring. You will probably find other benefits to keeping a journal as you write in it. You may also want to post your progress on social media and then have others join you there. Please let me know how you benefit as you take this journey. *Email me: sharonwpenn@gmail.com*

You Helping Others. Family members, friends, co-workers, and others will see the changes in you and may request your advice with a problem they have, or a behavior they want to change or enhance. You can then direct them to this book for guidance, or you can work together toward a goal. And you will be able to help them see it can be easy to make a change using these guides.

Changing. I don't mean to imply that change is easy, because it is not. Psychotherapist Dr. Margaret Click, who was a consultant on our research team said, "Change occurs through relearning, restructuring, redefining old, used, or even abused behaviors, thoughts, and feelings that progress from bad to good, unhealthy to healthy, from negative to positive positions."

Dr. Click continues, "In my opinion, whenever people are unhappy, they are holding on to a belief that no longer works for them, but they believe they are supposed to think that way, and this, in turn, creates conflict but rarely creates change. Most people are fearful of change in that they know what they already have and become anxious about the future with changes in the unknown."

Change creates more change. The research teams and individuals, testing the concepts that are the basis for this book, can tell you that changing your own behavior can cause a change in the people with whom you interact. Dr. Wayne Dyer, the author of 20 books and a self-development speaker, said in *The Power of Intention* (2004), "When you change the way you look at things, the things you look at change." I think that includes people changing their behavior toward you when your behavior changes toward them.

Isn't it a great concept to envision that the world can change when we work—person by person—to change, starting with ourselves? Anthropologist Margaret Mead, in *The Utne Reader* (1992) said, "Never doubt that a small group of thoughtful, committed people can change the world. Indeed, it is the only thing that ever has." You can be one of that group of thoughtful, committed people who will help to change the world by your efforts to change yourself and influence others!

I believe this book will make it easy for you to see how change can occur. There is no fear of change because you are going slowly and can see how small steps lead to big results. It is easy enough to try one small task toward a goal, and when you see how effective that change is and you see the positive results, you will be motivated to continue to the next task and onward to the next, ***one behavior at a time***.

IMPROVEMENT: "The joy of life is living it, or so it seems to me;
In finding shackles on your wrists, then struggling till you're free;
...The happiest mortal on the earth is he who ends his day
By leaving better than he found to bloom along the way..."
- Edgar Albert Guest *b. 1881, d. 1959*

Chapter 1

Mentally Healthy People

"As a single footstep will not make a path on the earth,
so a single thought will not make a pathway in the mind.
To make a deep physical path, we walk again and again.
To make a deep mental path, we must think over and over
the kind of thoughts we wish to dominate our lives."
H. David Thoreau

Good mental health is defined as a feeling of well-being in which a person knows his or her abilities, copes well with the normal stresses of life, works productively in his or her environment, and makes a contribution to the community.

Mental health is characterized by continuing personal growth, a sense of purpose in life, self-acceptance, and positive relations with others. Dr. Abraham Maslow, psychologist, called this concept "Self-Actualization."

Mental health providers have lists of behaviors they use to indicate when a person has mental well-being. Among those behaviors, people experience emotions freely but are not bowled over by them; take life's disappointments in stride; accept their shortcomings; get pleasure from easy, everyday things; have a tolerant, easy-going attitude; and can laugh at themselves. They can have satisfying and lasting personal relationships because they know how to give and receive love. In my research, I've found that mentally healthy people feel comfortable with themselves and others.

Other mental health providers also emphasize the role of environment in influencing well-being, as well as the traits listed above. They see mental health reflected in a person's overall happiness with the various areas of life: social relationships, work, family, and community life. The mentally healthy person knows how to adjust to their environment when necessary and also knows how to shape it.

Negative experiences in these areas can increase a person's stress level, and this, in turn, reduces their overall sense of well-being. Sources of negative stress include major life events: divorce; a spouse's, child's, or other loved one's suffering and death; job loss; and financial hardship, among others. Some people who experience traumatic events (war involvement, rape, and natural disasters, etc.) may also develop post-traumatic stress disorder (PTSD). Scientists are researching more PTSD cases with new findings and additional treatment modalities.

People may experience chronic stress when they face a continuing set of demands that can reduce their ability to function. Some of those demands are caregiving for elderly parents or a chronically ill relative, being a single parent, experiencing ongoing pain, financial hardship, unemployment, unresolved childhood issues, and other current problems. Many of these situations require the attention of a mental health professional; or, at least, a support group of like-minded people, with a professional leader.

In Orlando, there is *drop-in counseling* at *The Center,* a joint project with *Two Spirit Health Services. The Center,* at 946 N. Mills Avenue, is open Monday-Friday, noon-6 PM, and all are welcome with no questions asked. (Please call ahead for possible changes to the requirements: 407-228-8272). This service started in June 2016 for the LGBT community, when a terrorist killed 49 people and injured many more at an Orlando nightspot. This counseling would be an excellent service in many of our towns and cities because of trauma there. Search for this type of service in your area, and if not available, encourage mental health advocates to provide it. They can learn more about it from the Orlando-United Counseling program, started by the Mental Health Association of Central Florida. Call: 407-491-5643. *See Chapter Notes—Chapter 1 for more on services in Central Florida.*

You will find a checklist—Worksheet #1—at the end of this chapter to self-rate your well-being as you see it now. You can make copies of this assessment tool from the book if you want to rate yourself again as you work on some of the behaviors to improve your mental well-being if needed. From the worksheet, you will be able to determine what areas you are strong in and the areas you may want to change—one at a time. If you are unable to decide this alone, you may want to consult a mental health professional, or a close mentally-healthy friend or relative. Please contact me if you have questions. Email me: *sharonwpenn@gmail.com*

I have created posters for many of the behaviors addressed in this book which you can use as another reminder that you are making a change. You can print them from the book and post where you and others can see them. See the first one on the next page.

Sharon W. Penn

POSTER
MENTAL WELL-BEING
PENN'S DOs and DON'Ts

-DO HAVE A PURPOSE FOR YOUR LIFE.

-DO HAVE A POSITIVE ATTITUDE.

-DO HAVE GOOD RELATIONSHIPS.

-DO CONTINUE PERSONAL GROWTH.

-DO CONTROL YOUR OWN LIFE.

-DO KEEP OTHERS CLOSE.

-DO COPE WITH ADVERSITY.

-DO HAVE A SPIRITUAL LIFE.

-DO PHYSICAL ACTIVITIES.

-DO RELAXATION EXERCISES.

-DO MANAGE STRESS.

-DON'T NEGLECT YOUR HEALTH.

-DON'T FORGET-do one thing at a time.

Pick one and do it now.

Print and post where you and others will see it.

WORKSHEET 1

RATE YOUR MENTAL WELL-BEING

Please Note: *This test is designed for adults. Adolescent self-images are still forming; therefore, this assessment will not be accurate for them.*

Please use this scale to respond:

Never=1 **Rarely=2** **Sometimes=3**
Often=4 **Most of the time=5**

1-I have positive relationships with others. _____

2-I have a positive evaluation of myself. _____

3-I believe I control my life. _____

4-I think my life has purpose and meaning. _____

5-I have a balance of positive and negative emotions with work, family, and social life. _____

6-I manage my world pretty well. _____

7-I cope with stress. _____

8- I have a handle on how my family traits affect me. _____

9-I cope with adversity. _____

10-My family, friends, co-workers, neighbors, and others are there for me when I need them. _____

11-I work on staying healthy. _____

12-I do some form of physical activity several times a week—gardening, aerobics, walking, stretching, swimming, workout at a gym or home, dancing, weight-lifting, etc. _____

13-I practice relaxation techniques—meditation, music, television, yoga, reading, etc. _____

14-I have a spiritual life—prayer, bible study, church attendance, meditation, or other. _____

15-I work at continuing my personal growth and improving my life. _____

Add your numbers: Never ____ Rarely ____ Sometimes ____ Often ____ Most of the time ____ TOTAL_____

SCORING:
- If you scored 51-75, you have an extremely healthy mental well-being.
- If you scored 41-50, your score is average which is normal.
- If you scored 40 or less, your mental well-being can use some work.
- The good news is that you can improve your mental well-being. Notice where you answered Never, Rarely, or Sometimes to determine which behaviors you can start to work on, then check out Chapters 4 - 14 in the book for behaviors to change. Work on changing only one behavior at a time.
- Please consider seeing a mental health professional if your score is below 30.

Date_____   CHANGE 1 BEHAVIOR; IMPROVE YOUR LIFE
Sharon W. Penn 2017   Email me: *sharonwpenn@gmail.com*

Chapter 2

Why It's Hard to Change A Habit
And How to Do it Anyway

For the purpose of this chapter, the words
habit and behavior are used interchangeably.

By the time you are age three, your brain has formed thousands of connections per neuron. After the age of three the number of neuron connections in the brain *decreases* as we age (many remain dormant when not used). Why does this happen?

We learn by repetition, and that repetition carves deeper and permanent pathways in the brain. (Scientists call these pathways myelin—an electrical insulator that speeds the conduction of nerve impulses in the brain). So, a thread becomes a string becomes a rope becomes a chain. If we don't use it, we lose it.

Change is hard, but not impossible. You know this because the neural connections you don't use remain in the brain, though dormant. People, who exercise, read, play cards, or play word and computer games, i.e., keep mentally and physically active, can maintain their brain's flexibility. If you have lost some skills, you can always reactivate those neural pathways if you try, like bike riding or playing a musical instrument again after years of inactivity.

Change is hard, initially. While you may want to change your personality or life, at first it won't be easy because your brain is wired to do what it has been doing. You go back to old habits because the pathways are deeper from using them more.

We define a habit as an involuntary pattern of behavior, usually acquired by frequent repetition. Not all habits are bad; in fact, many habits are positive. We dress in the morning, tie our shoes, and write our names through the ease of habit. Some habits are annoying, ranging from nervous mannerisms and speech aberrations to smoking and overeating. See Chapter 2 Notes for a link to an article by Swati Salunkhe, career counselor.

Old habits fade away from not using them, but the underlying patterns remain in a dormant stage; so you have to be alert to make sure the unwanted habits don't rise up and gain prominence again.

To change a behavior or habit, you will have to form new neural pathways in the brain by doing some things differently, and once you have the new habits, you'll have to keep reinforcing them over and over.

Henry David Thoreau said it best, "As a single footstep will not make a path on the earth, so a single thought will not make a pathway in the mind. To make a deep physical path, we walk again and again. To make a deep mental path, we must think over and over the kind of thoughts we wish to dominate our lives." (This is so important I also included it in Chapter 1 and the Quotes, Chapter 15.)

Your goals to change a habit must be worthwhile and personal. They cannot be someone else's goals like those of your boss, parents, or even your spouse or partner. They cannot be suggestions from others about goals for you. They must be yours, and they must be of value to you. Tell yourself that you own your goals.

To change a habit, change the actions that produce it. If you usually get a snack like a big bag of popcorn whenever you sit down to watch a television show, decide to eat a small, low-cal snack before you sit down, and then take a glass of water to drink while you watch. Change the routine to help change the habit. It's all about being mindful of the habits you want to change.

Change the thought and you change the attitude, change the attitude and you change the resulting action. Attitude is the way we think or feel about a subject. You are the master of your attitudes; you have the choice to change them.

The following tips will help you put an end to your unwanted habits:

> **Recognize and isolate your unwanted habits.** You cannot overcome a habit until you become aware of it. Being mindful of it can help you stop doing it. In a small notebook or on the computer or smartphone, write down the habits you want to change. Then prioritize–pick one habit to work on first. When you've mastered that one, move on to the next habit you want to change. Change only one habit at the time.

> **Devise a replacement action.** Consciously choose to replace the thing that you know you shouldn't do with a practice that's right for you. Annoying habits are often a release for nervous tensions. If you're a knuckle-cracker, carry a small rubber ball— or even imagine you have one—and exercise your grip instead. A nail-biter can substitute clipping or filing fingernails rather than biting them. Have nail files nearby to use when you have a broken nail.

> A negative thinker can catch a thought and replace it with a positive one. Just say to yourself, "YES, I'm changing that thought." Overeaters can choose among several calorie-limiting methods; a brisk walk and a big glass of cool water can be a good substitute when you feel "the cravings."

> **Exercise is important for ending unwanted habits**. At the very least, give yourself 5-10 minutes a day of stretching and organized movement that includes breathing deeply. You can start out with 2-3 minutes and then work up to 10 or more minutes a day. Exercise is an excellent tool to help you break unwanted habits and it can make you feel more positive about yourself. You will become healthier, fitter, and calmer, and much less likely to fall back into those old annoying habits. If you do fall back, just start again.

> **A creative replacement hobby allows you to express yourself** through developing a new talent: gardening, playing music, writing books or articles, painting, drawing, acting, getting a pet, helping a shut-in, going to the gym, or finding volunteer programs to help others. Something new can be a welcome and refreshing diversion. Please tell me your success with changing habits. *Email me: sharonwpenn@gmail.com*

> **Use habit monitors.** Give yourself 5-10 minutes each day to reflect on the day, your relationships, and your progress in overcoming an unwanted habit. During the day, keep track of how many times the practice happens. What kinds of situations seem to bring it out? (This can be an excellent opportunity to write in your journal.)

> **You may need others to help remind you,** so inform your co-workers and family that you are attempting to break a particular habit. If you don't mind their help, ask them to tell you when they catch you falling into your old habit. And when they do, don't get annoyed. Make a point of thanking them each time they remind you; it helps you, and it also helps them feel good about themselves.

> **Seek experienced help from others.** Sometimes you need the advice and help of others who have overcome the same habit you wish to master. Occasionally, a psychologically damaging practice may even require professional help. However, many habits you can change yourself by the implementation of these suggestions. You can seek spiritual counsel and break any habit with God's help. "The things which are impossible with man are possible with God." (Luke 18:27-King James' version)

> **Start now.** Begin where you are to change a behavior today. Don't be like jokesters who say, "I must do something about procrastination—someday." Delay only reinforces the undesirable habit. You can change a habit easier today rather than tomorrow—so why wait?

The following are methods you can use to change a habit. Please read them over several times, try them, and then combine the tasks that work best for you:

- **To change a behavior, you must change your habits and way of thinking.** It helps to divide the changes you want to make into smaller objectives.

- **Clearly define each goal and make it measurable.** For example, if you want to reduce your weight, you may begin by deciding to cut calories then add exercise to a food plan; but this is not clearly defined (or measurable). It's better to state that you intend to cut 300 calories a day and walk or cycle for 5-30 (or more) minutes a day (which is measurable).

- **Divide the tasks into small, short-term sub-goals.** It's often easier to make small changes, one at a time, than large changes in your lifestyle. For example, to completely change your eating habits may seem insurmountable, but if you take one step at a time (e.g., cut down on sugary foods and snack foods by 50 percent), you'll notice that you've achieved much more than you first thought possible. This approach of making small, measurable alterations can be applied to almost anything you want to change.

- **Use affirmations & visualizations.** Write down in a 100 percent positive, confident manner the behavior you want to change. Every morning, noon, and before you go to bed, repeat an affirmation 10 or more times (examples: "I am losing two pounds a week," or "I am only speaking in positive terms"). Say it out loud or silently, then visualize performing your new habit—vividly imagine yourself, involving all your senses.

These simple methods will take only 10 to 15 minutes of your time, and it really can change your life. Please note: the more often you utilize your affirmations and visualizations, the faster you will see the results.

Affirmations can "rewire" the brain. Make them positive statements and in the now. Put them on colorful 3" x 5" index cards and place them near a mirror you use to say them to yourself every day.

Say your name as you look in the mirror and say the affirmations to yourself or aloud.

Here are examples to get you started:

"I am unique. Therefore I am awesome."

"I am happy to be me."

"Happiness is a choice. I base my happiness on my accomplishments and the blessings I have."

"Today I abandon my old habits and take up new, more positive ones."

"I love and accept myself."

"I am brimming with energy."

"I know I can do anything I decide to do."

Visualization is seeing your goal with your mind's eye. If you focus your visualization, and add more to the description, the faster the transformation will occur. Imagine every detail; the more the detail, the greater the focus, the more fervent you are, the more often you will apply visualization.

~ **Don't demand perfection from yourself.** You could, for example, when you first begin, choose to exercise 5-10 or more minutes a day, three to five days a week instead of 30 minutes a day, seven days a week. That goal gives you the possibility to succeed even if you don't manage to do it every day for a full 30 minutes. You can increase it as it becomes a habit, if you wish.

Reminder: Work on one habit at a time.

You can break bad habits! We are all creatures of habit. Swati Salunkhe said, "Change your habits, and you change your life." A habit or practice is like a cable; we weave a strand of it every day until it is tough to break. Some take longer than others to change, so be patient. With patience and diligence, the change will happen.

Now, decide which of the above statements you want to use to change a habit. Or you may want to choose these steps I've set up as Worksheet # 2:

Steps to Change a Habit

1-Clearly define the habit you want to change (your goal). The goal must be worthwhile to you—only you. Choose one goal at a time.
Example: Lose 10 pounds in five weeks.

2-Define how you will meet your goal.
Example: Choose a personal diet plan, e.g., DASH; Weight Watchers, Mediterranean, or another.

3-Make the goal measurable--State the number of times you will perform the new goal weekly; don't demand perfection.
Example: Perform the diet plan five days a week.

4-Divide tasks into small, short-term sub-goals.
Example: Lose two pounds weekly.

5-Identify replacement actions.
Example: Instead of snacking, go for a walk, call a friend, etc.

6-Write it down--put it on paper: the goal, tasks to meet the goal, replacement actions, affirmations, etc.
Example: Print these steps, or write them on colorful 3x5 cards to take with you and post at home. Read them often.

7-Choose an advisor. *Example: A support group, friend, diet buddy, fitness expert, or other.*

8-Use affirmations and visualizations. Change your thoughts, which change attitudes, which change actions—Say it & See it.
Example: "Each day my body becomes smaller and firmer."

9-Begin today; begin right now.

10-Keep a journal. Write down daily the changes you make, and the progress you see.

Give yourself a reward when your behavior change becomes a habit. Plan the reward as if you've already succeeded.

Steps to Change a Habit **is set up as Worksheet # 2**, located at the end of this chapter and in the Worksheet Section.

The only missing link is your commitment to implement the changes. Decide YOU are going to change a habit, then do it, one behavior at a time.

> "Whatever you can do, or dream you can do, begin it,
> Boldness has genius, power, and magic in it."
> Goethe

POSTER
HABIT CHANGE
PENN'S DOs and DON'Ts

~DO DEFINE EACH GOAL and MAKE IT MEASURABLE. Divide into smaller objectives.

~DO DIVIDE the TASKS into SUB-GOALS. Make small changes, one at a time.

~DO AFFIRMATIONS & VISUALIZATIONS. Say in a 100% positive manner what you will change.

~DO WRITE the NEW HABIT ON a 3X5 CARD. Keep it nearby as a reminder.

~DO DEVISE a REPLACEMENT ACTION. Replace the unwanted habit with one you want.

~DO USE HABIT MONITORS. Reflect each day on relationships and progress.

~DO ASK FOR HELP. Ask others to tell you when they see you falling into your old habits.

~DON'T DEMAND PERFECTION. Choose to exercise 3-5 days a week instead of 7 days a week.

~DON'T FORGET: DO ONLY ONE AT A TIME. BEGIN NOW!

Print and post where you and others will see it.

WORKSHEET 2

10 STEPS TO CHANGE A HABIT

**Do It Now;
Write It Here**

1~Clearly define the habit you want to change---
Example: Lose 10 pounds in five weeks.

2~Define how you will meet your goal---
Example: Choose a favorite diet plan.

3~Make the goal measurable---How many times?
Example: Perform the diet plan five days weekly.

4~Divide tasks into small, short-term sub-goals ---
Example: Lose two pounds weekly.

5~Identify replacement actions---
*Example: Instead of snacking, go for a walk,
call a friend, etc.*

6~Write it down---Put it on paper—the goal, tasks
to meet the goal, replacement actions,
affirmations, etc. Write on 3x5 cards.

7~Choose an advisor---
*Example: A support group, mentor, friend,
diet buddy, fitness expert, or other.*

8~Use affirmations and visualizations ---
Change your thoughts, which change attitudes,
which change actions—Say it & See it.
Example: "Each day my body becomes smaller and firmer."

9~Begin today. Put date here ---

10~Keep a journal. Write down changes and progress you see.

Chapter 3

Are You Addicted?

"We may think there is willpower involved, but more
likely... change is due to want power. Wanting the new
addiction more than the old one. Wanting the new me
in preference to the person I am now."
George A. Sheehan

The AUDIT is available at the end of this chapter, in the Worksheet Section, and is also available to take online.

Many people use the words habit and addiction interchangeably, but there are significant differences between the two. Habits may be positive or negative, and you may wish to make changes to some activity or behavior that you habitually do. But, you may not be addicted to it. When you are addicted to something that has an adverse impact on your life or health, it is advisable or even necessary to seek professional treatment. So, discerning between the two words is important.

How are the words habit and addiction similar? Both types are the result of activity that you do on a regular basis. Researchers have found that a habit begins when we perform any action repeatedly in response to a cue, such as brushing our teeth after a meal. The action then becomes encoded in the brain as an automatic response to that cue.

With addiction, we initially choose our behavior—we voluntarily light up, go online, or pour the glass of alcohol—and as we repeat the activity, the behavior becomes the habit that forms neurologically with powerful dopamine rewards. Many everyday activities stimulate dopamine release: shopping, gambling, exercise, sex, eating tasty food, social engagement, to name just a few.

When we use substances for a significant dose of dopamine, then we want to continue using it for the "feel-good" effect. This ultimate reward creates the addiction. Then, an extreme craving is the result when an addicted person does not get his or her substance.

Are you addicted? If you drink alcohol, you may be wondering if you are addicted and if you need to seek treatment. If you haven't done so already, and you wonder if you are addicted, please take the AUDIT at the end of this chapter, in the Worksheet Section, or online. *http://www.addictionandrecovery.org/addiction-self-test-html*

Note: It can be difficult for a person to determine, on his or her own, if an addiction is present, and so, they need to seek professional guidance and advice on this matter if they suspect they are addicted.

If you question the possibility that you are addicted or are becoming addicted to a substance such as drugs or alcohol, or you are concerned about someone else, you can seek guidance and support at a local center. http://www.addiction.com
Call: 1-877-671-1785.

National Council on Alcoholism and Drug Dependence Inc. 1-800-622-2255 This resource has self-assessment tests for alcohol use and drug abuse. *Go online: www.ncadd.org to take the tests and get immediate test results.* There are numerous articles about both alcohol and drug abuse for parents, friends & family, and youth at this website.

NIH-National Institute on Drug Abuse: The Science of Drug Abuse & Addiction *www.drugabuse.gov* A ton of information is found here with directions to other resources.

TREATMENT HUB 365--Search to find addiction and mental health treatment options in your area. Then make online appointments directly: clinics, doctors, therapists, counselors, treatment centers and hospitals of your choice. *www.treatmenthub365.com*

There are many resources available online. Or use this website: *http://alcoholrehabdepot.com*

PLEASE NOTE: The AUDIT, which follows on the next pages, *may seem like an easy test to fail. If you applied this test to other aspects of your life you would almost certainly come up as being addicted to something. For example, most people watch too much television or eat too much of their favorite food. But those are so-called "soft addictions," and the AUDIT questionnaire was not designed to assess them. It is extremely reliable when it comes to assessing alcohol addiction. Babor*

WORKSHEET 3

THE AUDIT TEST FOR
ALCOHOL ADDICTION (ALCOHOLISM)

AUDIT (**A**lcohol **U**se **D**isorders **I**dentification **T**est) (10 questions) was developed by the World Health Organization (WHO). The test correctly classifies 95% of people into either alcoholics or non-alcoholics. Permission is given to print the test in this book, or **you can take it online.** *http://www.addictionandrecovery.org/addiction-self-test-html*

To correctly answer some of these questions you need to know the definition of a drink.

For this test one drink is:

One can of beer (12 oz or approx 330 ml of 5% alcohol), or

One glass of wine (5 oz or approx 140 ml of 12% alcohol), or

One shot of liquor (1.5 oz or approx 40 ml of 40% alcohol).

___1. How often do you have a drink containing alcohol?

Never (score 0)

Monthly or Less (score 1)

2-4 times a month (score 2)

2-3 times a week (score 3)

4 or more times a week (score 4)

___2. How many alcoholic drinks do you have on a typical day when you are drinking?

1 or 2 (0)

3 or 4 (1)

5 or 6 (2)

7-9 (3)

10 or more (4)

___3. How often do you have 6 or more drinks on one occasion?

Never (0)

Less than monthly (1)

Monthly (2)

Weekly (3)

Daily or almost daily (4)

___4. How often during the past year have you found that you drank more or for a longer time than you intended?
Never (0)
Less than monthly (1)
Monthly (2)
Weekly (3)
Daily or almost daily (4)

___5. How often during the past year have you failed to do what was normally expected of you because of your drinking?
Never (0)
Less than monthly (1)
Monthly (2)
Weekly (3)
Daily or almost daily (4)

___6. How often during the past year have you had a drink in the morning to get yourself going after a heavy drinking session?
Never (0)
Less than monthly (1)
Monthly (2)
Weekly (3)
Daily or almost daily (4)

___7. How often during the past year have you felt guilty or remorseful after drinking?
Never (0)
Less than monthly (1)
Monthly (2)
Weekly (3)
Daily or almost daily (4)

___8. How often during the past year have you been unable to remember what happened the night because of your drinking?
Never (0)
Less than monthly (1)
Monthly (2)
Weekly (3)
Daily or almost daily (4)

___9. Have you or anyone else been injured as a result of your drinking?
No (0)
Yes, but not in the past year (2)
Yes, during the past year (4)

___10. Has a relative, friend, doctor, or health care worker been concerned about your drinking, or suggested that you cut down?
No (0)
Yes, but not in the past year (2)
Yes, during the past year (4)

Your score: _____

If you scored 8-10 or more, you are probably addicted to alcohol. Please see a professional counselor for a full assessment.

PLEASE NOTE: The AUDIT, may seem like an easy test to fail. If you applied this test to other aspects of your life you would almost certainly come up as being addicted to something. For example, most people watch too much television or eat too much of their favorite food. But those are so-called "soft addictions," and the AUDIT questionnaire was not designed to assess them. It is extremely reliable when it comes to assessing alcohol addiction. Babor

Chapter 4

Behavior Change: Convey Your Approachability

How do we convey to others that we can be easily approached and are friendly and receptive to their presence? Some people seem to have a straightforward manner that helps us reach out to them. We all know someone who is warm and congenial, and it appears to come naturally to them. Then others have to work at it. This chapter will help those people who want to communicate that they are open to having others enter their space.

In this chapter, seven behaviors will help you become more approachable:

1. Smile appropriately
2. Make eye contact
3. Greet people and get a response
4. Touch people: shake hands, hug, or touch the arm
5. Use positive, open body language
6. Compliment people
7. Say the person's name in conversation.

Choose a favorite to begin. It's not necessary to practice the behaviors the way they are presented; in fact, you may want to start with the easiest one for you. Then, some people like a challenge, so they will want to start with the hardest behavior for them to change, giving them a greater feeling of accomplishment when they master the behavior change. If you're doing this change with another person or a group, it may be helpful to work on the same behavior so you can practice with them.

Start with your chosen behavior, and when it becomes a habit, pick another and work on it while continuing to practice the one(s) you've done previously. Once these seven become habits, and therefore effortless, you won't have to think about doing them, so practice all of them each day as they become habits to keep them active. The behaviors then become ingrained and part of your life. Please let me know if changing these behaviors has changed your life as I expect it will. *Email me: sharonwpenn@gmail.com*

Start small. Choose one or two people a day to approach until you're up to five or more a day.

1-Smile appropriately. The easiest behavior to show others you are approachable is a smile. We all do it, but maybe not often enough. It's probably the most natural action to start or increase your use of a behavior change.

Anna, a member of the first research team I led, said her mother began noticing that the corners of her mouth were always turned down when she would see herself in a mirror. She decided that it made her look older and unhappy. She made an effort to keep her mouth turned upward so she would look happy. At her mother's funeral, many people told Anna they always thought of her mother as being a very happy and content woman.

Of course, some people have a harder time smiling at others, so if you're one of the people who doesn't smile naturally, begin by practicing in front of a mirror. When you go to the bathroom and wash your hands, give your face in the mirror a big smile. A happy-face sticker there can remind you. Another way to practice is to have a mirror near your computer or desk and smile at it every chance you get to look up from your work, email, or games. And when you make or take a telephone call, smile as you say hello; it is reported to be detectable to the recipient. Also, for the same reason, you can smile when you leave a recorded message for someone.

Another way to practice the behavior change is to smile at children and pets. They are the easiest reminder that you are going to practice your smile, and generally, the children will smile back—up until they reach a certain age, that is. If you work in an office and have display space, put up photographs of children and pets having fun. It will not only help you remember to smile, but it will also be an excellent ice-breaker with others.

You have to know when to smile and when not to smile. When Christy, with our research team, began the project to change her behaviors to become more approachable, she practiced her smile on her husband, but maybe sometimes at the wrong time. On one or two occasions, when she smiled as they were having a serious discussion; her husband very solemnly said, "This is not funny."

> *A SMILE costs nothing but gives much.*
> *It enriches those who receive,*
> *without making poorer those who give…*
> Unknown Author

2-Make eye contact. This behavior change may be a bit harder than putting on a smile. People in different professions learn a different method of looking at others. Jennie, with the research team, experienced several times being correctly identified as a teacher because of the manner that she had as a teacher of looking into students' eyes. In her case, this behavior carried over into her social skills with adults.

This same skill came in handy while traveling in another country. Jennie became aware of a man following her and her female traveling companion much too closely. In a quiet voice, she warned her friend of what was happening, and then abruptly stopped, turned to the man and stared him in the eyes. He quickly turned and continued walking, this time, away from them.

Culturally, people are vastly different in their eye contact behavior. In Japan, I'm told, listeners are taught to focus on a speaker's neck to avoid eye contact. Different groups exhibit various methods of eye contact, and in some cases, no eye contact at all. Is it any wonder, in our melting pot of a world, we are confused as we struggle to interpret the behavior of people of other races and cultures when they attempt to communicate with us?

Some researchers define eye contact as sometimes not looking directly into someone's eyes, but close to the eyes during a conversation. The speaker usually has a decrease of eye contact and the listener has an eye contact increase. We need to learn to *increase* eye contact when we speak so we can build rapport.

When I was counseling couples, I sometimes had them sit facing each other with knees touching. I would ask them to look into each other's eyes and breathe slowly. They were to hold the eye contact for as long as they could. After about 5 to 10 minutes, one of them would break the connection. We would then talk about how they felt when they were holding the eye contact. At first, they were uncomfortable but became more relaxed in subsequent sessions. When they did continue the practice at home, some of them reported a sense of absorbing the other person's energy. The counseling clients who were able to continue the practice away from my office said they felt closer and more in tune with their partner than before the exercise; it just took practice to be comfortable doing it.

You might try this eye-contact exercise with a partner or a close friend. Notice if you feel a sense of exposure or vulnerability. Notice what your natural reaction is. Do you feel vulnerable, impatient, anxious, silly, what? You may want to draw back, but keep looking into the other person's eyes. If you look away, notice what came up that caused you to break contact. Over time, did it become more comfortable? Did you talk together after the exercise ended? Did you feel closer to each other? I'd like to hear about your experience.

Email me: sharonwpenn@gmail.com

3-Greet people and get a response—"Here comes that salesperson-type with a bigger-than-life smile and a hand struck out to shake mine. How do I get out of this?" Is that how you feel when someone heads toward you a little too enthusiastically? When a person reaches out to shake someone's hand, it encroaches on their personal space (about arm's length). We want to be friendly, but we have to find that stopping spot—their space—so that we don't overpower a person and see the wariness in their eyes when we come near.

Salespeople receive training on how to greet customers which is an excellent guide on how we can welcome people in everyday situations. Trainers tell us we need a positive mind as we approach people, if possible. Positive mental pictures can help us put a bit of pep in our step as we greet someone. To have our words heard by others, they need to be confident, positive, enthusiastic, and humorous, if appropriate. How we greet people needs to be heartfelt and not seem forced.

4-Touch people appropriately. "For human beings, you need two hugs a day to survive, four hugs for maintenance, six hugs to grow," said Virginia Satir, a family therapist in the '70s. Studies done in the 1950s of institutionalized children showed that, even though the children received proper physical care and good nutrition, they became sickly years afterward. As babies and children, they allegedly were not picked up and held or hugged. They suffered from a lack of tender, loving care.

Hugging usually makes everyone feel good. It's a way to show a person that you care about them. Do you notice how people smile when they even observe someone being hugged? And you often hear someone who is being hugged say, "That feels so good." *Note: Always ask permission to give a hug.*

Have you noticed how touch seems to be healing? When someone feels bad, talking may not help a lot, but touch helps us relax and feel better. In fact, I think hugging each other should be a *supervised* practice in all orphanages, nursing homes, retirement centers, and some other institutions. Do you agree? Please tell me.
Email me: sharonwpenn@gmail.com

5-Use positive, open body language. Nonverbal communication provides us with a model for conveying messages without the use of verbal language. Body positions, both open and closed, send messages to others. As expected, research finds that individuals with open body positions are perceived more positively and are more influential than those with closed body positions. And research shows that people who lean their body forward increase the verbal output of their partner more than those who do not.

Adopting or imitating common bodily positions (identified as posture matching) by people in pairs or groups tend to enhance rapport between/among the participants because it signals that they are open to and in sync with one another. The adoption of *non-congruent* postures does just the opposite. They tend to indicate attitudinal and perceptual differences or relationship distances.

Here are some more research findings that are worth remembering when you are practicing open body language to be more approachable to others:

- Individuals' *hand movements*, especially vertical movements, can indicate a positive interpersonal relationship.
- Listeners who engage in *head-nodding* provide positive reinforcements for speakers, and probably increase the duration of the speech.

6-Compliment people. Among friends, family members, acquaintances, and co-workers, compliments are often exchanged upon greeting or in the middle of a conversation. These compliments show us that people are paying attention to each other and have noticed small changes or extra efforts the person took, i.e., in his or her appearance. It is appropriate to offer compliments about new hairstyles, clothing, and other appearance.

Many of us also believe in reinforcing self-esteem by complimenting people on the things that are important to them. We compliment children on their appearance, schoolwork, their athletic ability, or their music and artistic talents. We compliment adults on their appearance, home, yard, car, or cooking.

We can use compliments as a way of initiating conversation or bringing up something we have in common with the person to whom we are speaking. Complimenting someone on their home or cooking may start a conversation about home décor or favorite recipes.

Please note: *Some people are sensitive to personal compliments from members of the opposite sex--or even the same sex—when they are in a position of authority over them. Sexual harassment has become an issue in the workplace, so managers will want to be cautious—focus more on the performance you can appreciate than on the physical things.*

7-Say the person's name in conversation. This may be the most difficult behavior to change because of our fear that if we try to call someone by name, we may forget and then we will be so embarrassed! Only a few people can call others *Honey, Darling*, or *Sweetie* all the time and get away with it.

Everyone has problems remembering names, at least once in awhile. Sometimes you can forget a person's name even when you know them well. So what's the way to handle this embarrassment? Just laugh and make a joke out of it. When you pair a light joke with an apology, you're probably going to be forgiven immediately because that person has probably also forgotten names. If you forget a name while introducing someone, don't make a big deal about it, and apologize later.

Remembering names is a skill you can acquire. Here are a few ideas:

- ~ Use the person's name immediately in conversation after an introduction.
- ~ Quickly introduce that new person to someone else you know.
- ~ If you don't have an opportunity to speak up directly, you can find a word association with the individual's name.
- ~ Jot down the person's name, if possible.
- ~ Ask for a business card, if appropriate.
- ~ Listen, listen, and listen.

(More help for remembering names is located
in Chapter 11 about Memory.)

Now, you have new skills to improve ways to communicate your approachability. To help you remember, I've created a poster you can print and post for you and others to see. If you decide to try this behavior change, there is a checklist and a contract to sign to remind yourself of your commitment to this goal. On the last pages of this chapter is a worksheet for a quick look at the tasks to improve your approachability: Put these tasks to work—one day, one skill at a time.

POSTER
APPROACHABILITY
PENN'S DOs and DON'Ts

PRACTICE DAILY ON 2-10 PEOPLE:

- DO SMILE APPROPRIATELY.

- DO MAKE EYE CONTACT.

- DO GREET and GET A RESPONSE.

- DO TOUCH APPROPRIATELY.

- DO SHOW OPEN BODY LANGUAGE.

- DO COMPLIMENT PEOPLE.

- DO SAY PEOPLE'S NAME IN CONVERSATION.

- DO ONE BEHAVIOR AT A TIME until they all become habits.

- DON'T STOP *until they all become habits. Soon, you will have mastered all of them. Please tell me about your experiences. Email me: sharonwpenn@ gmail.com*

Print and post where you and others will see it.

CHECKLIST & CONTRACT

I WILL COMPLETE THIS CHECKLIST & CONTRACT
FOR EACH BEHAVIOR I WORK ON.

____ I am motivated to change/improve my behavior:
Name Behavior: **Convey My Approachability.**

____ I will begin by working to improve one behavior at a time.

____ I will complete this checklist for each behavior.

____ I will sign a contract and place it where I can see it often.

____ I will work with another person to improve this behavior.

____ I will keep a journal about my progress and feelings.

____ I will read Chapters 1 & 2.

____ I will complete the worksheets for Chapters 1 & 2.

____ I will read the chapter of the behavior I want to improve.

____ I will complete the worksheet(s) relevant to this behavior.

CONTRACT

As of today, I choose to improve my life, 1 behavior at a time, by **Conveying My Approachability.**

Name_____   Date_____

Print and Post

WORKSHEET 4

APPROACHABILITY CHECKLIST

7 Tasks-1 a day   Times Tried 2-10 times daily

1-Smile Appropriately ---

2-Eye Contact ---

3-Greet/Get Response ---

4-Touch Appropriately ---

5-Open Body Language ---

6-Compliment People ---

7-Say Name in Conversation ---

Please start out by doing one of these behaviors, one at a time with 2-10 people, until it becomes a habit. Then, go to another behavior until it becomes a habit. Soon, you will have mastered all of them. Please tell me about your experiences.
Email me: sharonwpenn@gmail.com

Chapter 5

Behavior Change: Boost Your Self-Esteem

"Never forget that you are one of a kind. And never forget, no matter how overwhelming life's challenges and problems seem to be, that one person can make a difference in the world. In fact, it is always because of one person that all changes that matter in the world come about. So be that one person."
Buckminster Fuller, author

What is self-esteem and how do we get it? We usually know when we've got it, and when we don't. Knowing *how* to get it when we don't have it is more elusive. *What?* You don't always know when you've got it? Just feeling good about yourself is one indicator.

When you can answer "Yes, often" to these questions, then you can be confident that your self-esteem is high:

- *Are you honest with your feelings when dealing with others?*
- *Are you making an attempt to resolve issues in your life?*
- *Do you volunteer to help others who are needier?*
- *Do you have good eye contact with others?*
- *Are you compassionate of other's plights in life?*

Your self-esteem may be low when you answer "Yes, often" to these:

- *Do you anger quickly and is your anger often inappropriate?*
- *Are you a smoker or overeater, or do you abuse alcohol or drugs?*
- *Are you often ill with colds or other minor illnesses?*
- *Do you often tell lies or a half-truth?*
- *Do you see yourself as a victim, or feel victimized by other people's actions?*

Your answers to these types of questions may vary from day-to-day, according to Margaret Click, Ph.D., in her article, "Self-Esteem." She says, "It is easy to feel worthy and good about ourselves when things are going well. The trick is to have the seeds of the positive self-love, self-image, and self-awareness so deeply planted and well-fertilized within us that we feel worthy, compassionate, and loving toward ourselves even when, and especially when events are not going well."

The good news is that you can boost your self-esteem, so you are prepared for those times when you have a setback. When the boosters become habits, then you are fortified and prepared for any event that happens in your life.

So, if you think your self-esteem needs boosting, try these tips—one at a time—for starters:

Do something every day that you do extremely well. It may seem insignificant, but any accomplishment bolsters self-esteem. It may be something as simple as working a crossword puzzle, or cooking a dish you're famous for and sharing it with a neighbor or co-worker, or finding a new activity you like to share with your family or friends.

Learn something new every day. It may be as easy as learning a new word that you read in the morning paper or heard on the evening news. You may read something new that you want to share with your spouse or partner, child, or co-worker. The more you know, the more interesting you can be.

Do something that helps you feel good about yourself. It may be something easy like playing a sport you're good at, buying a new outfit, or getting a manicure or pedicure. You can try a walk or an exercise workout with high-energy music. Whatever helps, do it.

Cultivate people whose accomplishments you admire. Men and women who have succeeded at something—be it head of a company, a top producer in sales, or someone who has a great relationship with their partner or children—may have secrets they are usually happy to share. They will probably be receptive to friendly overtures and welcome your interest and admiration of them.

Don't allow anyone to put you down. No matter who it is, the relationship isn't worth it if it makes you miserable. Tell the person exactly what bothers you; if there's no change, say "goodbye." Don't let anyone upset your life. Definitely walk away if you're dealing with a bully, and get protection if you feel you are in danger. And if *you* are putting yourself down—stop it! *Critical thoughts destroy self-esteem as effectively as positive thoughts build it.*

Concentrate on the things you like about yourself. Find something that people comment on about you, and then play it up. Whatever your specialty is—be it hair, eyes, smile, creative ability, a talent, a unique skill, personality, or other—use it freely and often. And think about it anytime you are feeling down.

If you can change the things about yourself that bother you—do it now. If you need to lose weight; quit smoking; start exercising; get out of debt; move to another job; or treat loved ones, co-workers, and others with more respect—do it. And, do it *now*—one day, one step at a time.

If what bothers you is something you can't do anything about— your height, race, origin, or some other unalterable state—stop brooding about it. Get on with your life. Seek out information about famous people who have the same trait, reminding yourself that it didn't keep them down, so it can help you, too.

Give thanks. And, most of all, think often about things that you're grateful for. This helps you know how special you are. Keeping a daily gratitude journal helps you focus on your blessings; you will be more mindful as you think about what will go into your journal. You can use a spiral notebook or a fancy bound book to write in, or use the computer or your smartphone to record your thoughts.

Self-esteem is based on your thoughts, feelings, and beliefs about yourself. You can do something when you believe you can, and when you tell yourself you can't do something, you increase your chance of failure. The next time you're up against a challenge, think positive thoughts for success.

> "Whether you think you can or
> you think you can't—you're right."
> Henry Ford

Sharon W. Penn

POSTER
BOOST YOUR SELF-ESTEEM
PENN'S DOs and DON'Ts

~ DO SOMETHING EVERY DAY THAT YOU DO WELL.

~ DO LEARN A NEW THING EVERY DAY.

~ DO WHAT MAKES YOU FEEL GOOD.

~ DO ASSOCIATE WITH PEOPLE YOU ADMIRE.

~ DO BE HONEST WITH OTHERS.

~ DO HELP NEEDY PEOPLE.

~ DO RESOLVE ISSUES IN YOUR LIFE.

~ DON'T TELL LIES or HALF-TRUTHS.

~ DON'T SMOKE, OVEREAT, or ABUSE ALCOHOL or DRUGS.

~ DON'T BE VICTIMIZED BY OTHERS.

~ DON'T NEGLECT YOUR HEALTH.

~ DON'T FORGET-change only one thing at a time.

Print and post where you and others will see it.

CHECKLIST & CONTRACT

I WILL COMPLETE THIS CHECKLIST & CONTRACT FOR EACH BEHAVIOR I WORK ON.

____ I am motivated to change/improve my behavior:
Name Behavior: **Boosting My SELF-ESTEEM.**

____ I will begin by working to improve one behavior at a time.

____ I will complete this checklist for my behavior improvement.

____ I will sign a contract and place it where I can see it often.

____ I will work with another person to improve this behavior.

____ I will keep a journal about my progress and feelings.

____ I will read Chapters 1 & 2.

____ I will complete the worksheets for Chapters 1 & 2.

____ I will read the chapter of the behavior I want to improve.

____ I will complete the worksheet(s) relevant to this chapter.

CONTRACT

As of today, I choose to improve my life, one behavior at a time, by **Boosting My SELF-ESTEEM.**

Name_____   Date_____

Print and Post

WORKSHEET 5A

SELF-ESTEEM SURVEY

Please respond to the questions using the following scale:

Never=1 **Rarely=2** **Sometimes=3**

Often=4 **Most of the time=5**

Do you make eye contact with others? _____

Do you volunteer to help needy people? _____

Are you honest with your feelings when dealing with other? _____

Did you feel loved as a child? _____

Do you feel loved now? _____

Do you avoid smoking or overeating? _____

Do you avoid abusing alcohol or drugs? _____

Are you free of colds, flu, and other illnesses? _____

Do you choose not to be angry? _____

If you do become angry, do you tell the person how you feel in a non-threatening way? _____

Do you speak your mind when an issue comes up about which you have strong feelings? _____

Do you avoid telling lies or half-truths? _____

Do you take risks? _____

Are you compassionate of others? Yes _____ No_____

TOTAL YOUR POINTS _____

YOUR TOTAL POINTS _____

If your total points for the Self-Esteem Survey are:

50-70 – You have excellent self-esteem.

42-49 - Good; can use some work.

41 and below - Work on building your self-esteem by reading and practicing the habits in Chapter 5.

WORKSHEET 5B

SELF-ESTEEM REVIEW

Please make copies so you can do the review often. You can use this as a progress report. Review the statements once a week, and later, once a month to see how your self-esteem is changing. Keep the worksheets in a folder or on your computer.

DATE _____

- Things I Do Well:

- Positive Ways I Share Feelings:

- Skills I Have:

- Talents I Have:

- Ways I'm Learning to Take Care of Myself:

- Ways I'm Making Positive Changes:

- Personal Characteristics that Help Me to Grow and Change:

Sharon W. Penn 2017 Change 1 Behavior, Improve Your Life.
Email me: sharonwpenn@gmail.com

Chapter 6

Behavior Change:
Try The Blues Busters

"If you always do what you've always done,
you'll always get what you've always gotten."
Jessie Potter

Depression can start in many ways. Most major life events, e.g., separation or divorce, a loved one's death, job loss, and financial hardship, among others, can cause situational depression. Other people suffer from more extreme traumatic events, war involvement, rape, natural disasters, etc. Some people have a genetic form of depression. Stanford Medicine says scientists look at patterns of illness in families to estimate their "heritability," or roughly what percentage of their cause is due to genes. They have a website with details about forms of depression. See Chapter 6 Chapter Notes.

If you believe you have a severe depressive condition, please see a mental health provider, NOW. There is a self-assessment test at the end of this chapter for you to take to determine if you may be depressed.

Also, try some easy-to-do activities to decrease a mild depression. Just pick a favorite—one a day. Get started now. You can then add others. Action is the key. These tasks are in a checklist at the end of this chapter.

Take a walk. Or try another regular exercise or yoga, preferably with people you like. Well-being produced by exercise is probably due to the release of endorphins, the body's natural painkiller. Regular exercise also raises your metabolism, which energizes you. Exercising with other people does two things: socializing discourages isolation, and it can help assure you will continue the program.

Schedule social events. Go to a ball game, a funny movie, a concert, or participate in a sport. Discover what you enjoy doing and make time for it. Also, it's much more fun when you do it with people you like.

Work at having close, loving relationships. Research has shown that of all the characteristics that happy people share, loving relationships seem to be the most important. Pay special attention to the people you love. And, yes, you do have to work at it.

Create successes for yourself. Start a new project, or get a fresh start on a long-delayed chore or finish one. Sometimes, just the act of starting something new or finalizing it can give you a feeling of pleasure. "Whatever you can do, or dream you can do, begin it. Boldness has genius, power, and magic in it." Goethe

Help someone in need—a disadvantaged child, a homeless person, and the elderly. Or cook a dish or a meal for a neighbor, friend, or co-worker. It's possible that altruism builds happiness in two ways: it enhances self-esteem and may relieve both physical and mental stress. Also, you'll enjoy the feeling of helping someone else feel good.

Treat yourself to pleasures. Eat a favorite food, take a hot bath, buy some flowers, read an uplifting book. Use this as a reward, a change of pace, or just when you need a lift. Remind yourself often you are special and deserve the best. Self-talk is important, and it also helps that when you do self-talk, call yourself by name while looking in the mirror as you say the affirmation. (At the end of this chapter there are examples of affirmations, and you can add your own.)

Get out your coloring book: Coloring is a low-stress activity that allows a person to unlock their creative potential. It also helps relieve tension and pent-up anxiety because it opens memories of childhood and simpler times. Some mental health counselors recommend it as a relaxation technique and believe it helps us to enter a more creative, freer state. They suggest we try it in a quiet environment, or with pleasant music. Let the colors and the lines flow. If you are having a bad day, then take out some crayons or colored pencils and start coloring.

Express appreciation. EVERY DAY give someone a compliment--a warm fuzzy. Choose a family member, a co-worker, a service worker, or a friend, and tell them something that makes them unique to you and others. Or write a letter to a person from your past who was important in your life. Or write a thank-you note to someone you've heard of who has helped people in the community. You can do some of this online if you have an email address or use social media.

Write in a gratitude journal EVERY DAY. Writing in the journal helps you see all the positive things around you that you might have missed if you weren't looking for them. Write things you are grateful for on your computer or smartphone, or in a spiral notebook, or on 3 x 5 index cards. To keep it interesting, share in social media and others can share with you.

Make time for prayer and meditation EVERY DAY. One recent study found that participating in regular meditation, prayer, or another spiritual practice thickens parts of the brain, and could be the reason those activities tend to guard against depression, especially in those at risk for the disorder.

Researchers found that people who expect answers to their prayers are less likely to experience anxiety-relevant disorders like worry, fear, self-consciousness, social anxiety, and obsessive-compulsive behavior, compared to people who pray but don't expect to receive any comfort or protection from God.

Take one step at a time EVERY DAY. Out of the dumps and on to that great feeling. Choose one activity and when you do that one, notice immediately that you begin to feel better. If it seems like a lot to do, just try one a week until you feel better; then do one a day.

If your depression is mild, these actions are guaranteed to lift your mood. If the depression is due to a life event like job loss or loss of a loved one, it will take time for the depression to lift. Having a trusted friend or relative, or a support group you can talk with can help.

If the Blues hang on for more than a few months, you may have more than a case of the blues; it could be a severe depression. You can still do the Blues Busters, but please see a mental health professional or your family doctor right away. Help is available.

A good therapist can teach you new skills for living a more productive and satisfying life.

**DON'T DELAY; GET MOVING,
AND ENJOY LIFE AGAIN**

Affirmations are proven methods of self-improvement. They can "rewire" the brain. Make them confident statements and in the now. Put them on 3 x 5 index cards and place them near a mirror you will use to say them to yourself every day. Say your name as you look in the mirror and say the affirmations to yourself. You can write your own, or try these:

"I am unique. Therefore I am awesome."

"I am happy and proud to be me."

"Creative energy leads me to new ideas."

"Happiness is a choice. I base my happiness on my accomplishments and the blessings I have."

"Today I abandon my old habits and take up new, more positive ones."

"I have achieved greatness."

"I love and accept myself for the person I am."

"I am brimming with energy."

"I am overflowing with joy."

"I believe I can do everything."

"I forgive anyone who has hurt me."

POSTER
BLUES BUSTERS
Penn's DOs and DON'Ts

~DO YOGA, TAKE A WALK, or EXERCISE.

~DO SCHEDULE SOCIAL EVENTS.

~DO WORK at HAVING CLOSE, LOVING RELATIONSHIPS.

~DO CREATE SUCCESSES FOR YOURSELF.

~DO HELP SOMEONE IN NEED.

~DO TREAT YOURSELF to PLEASURE.

~DO EXPRESS APPRECIATION.

~DO WRITE in a GRATITUDE JOURNAL.

~DO PRAY and MEDITATE.

~DON'T FORGET: TAKE ONE STEP at a TIME.

Print and post where you and others will see it.

CHECKLIST & CONTRACT

I WILL COMPLETE THIS CHECKLIST & CONTRACT
FOR EACH BEHAVIOR I WORK ON.

____ If I am depressed every day, for most of the day, I will immediately call a mental health provider or my doctor.

____I am motivated to change/improve my behavior:

Name Behavior: Try THE BLUES BUSTERS.

____ I begin by working to improve one behavior at a time.

____ I will complete this checklist for my behavior improvement.

____ I will sign a contract and place it where I can see it often.

____ I will work with another person to improve this behavior.

____ I will keep a journal about my progress and feelings.

____ I will read Chapters 1 & 2.

____ I will complete the worksheets for Chapters 1 & 2.

____ I will read the chapter of the behavior I want to improve.

____ I will complete the worksheet(s) relevant to this behavior.

CONTRACT

As of today, I choose to improve my life, one behavior at a time, by **Trying THE BLUES BUSTERS.**

Name_____ Date_____

Print and Post

55

WORKSHEET 6A

DEPRESSION SCALE

**Please use this scale to respond for how you have felt
during the past two weeks:**

Never=1   **Rarely=2**   **Sometimes=3**
         Often=4   **Most of the time=5**

I have a poor appetite or I overeat. ____

I have insomnia or I oversleep. ____

I have low energy or fatigue. ____

I have low self-esteem. ____

I have poor concentration. ____

I have difficulty making decisions. ____

I have feelings of hopelessness. ____

I have little interest or pleasure in anything. ____

I feel depressed. ____

I feel suicidal. ____

Total Score _____

If your score is 40 or more; or if you feel suicidal or depressed for most of the day,
more days than not, please see a mental health provider or your medical doctor NOW.

MENTAL HEALTH CRISIS HOTLINE
1-800-553-4539 or 1-888-269-4389

If you feel suicidal, or if you have five or more of the other nine symptoms on this Depression Scale during the same 2-week period; and at least one of the symptoms is either depressed mood or loss of interest or pleasure, please seek professional help, now. DSM-5

Depression (major depressive disorder) is a common and serious medical illness that negatively affects how you feel, the way you think and how you act. Fortunately, it is also treatable. Depression causes feelings of sadness and/or a loss of interest in activities once enjoyed. It can lead to a variety of emotional and physical problems and can decrease a person's ability to function at work and home. DSM-5

See Chapter 6 for information on DSM-5.

WORKSHEET 6B

BLUES BUSTERS CHECKLIST

Choose one each day until it becomes a habit:

1-Take a walk, exercise, or do yoga…

2-Schedule a social event…

3-Have close, loving relationships…

4-Create successes for yourself…

5-Help someone in need…

6-Treat yourself to pleasures…

7-Get out your coloring book…

8-EVERY DAY: express appreciation…

9-EVERY DAY: write in a gratitude journal…

10-EVERY DAY: pray & meditate…

11-EVERY DAY: take one step at a time…

Sharon W. Penn 2017 Change 1 Behavior, Improve Your Life.
Email me: sharonwpenn@gmail.com

Chapter 7

Behavior Change:
Manage Your Anger

Before you read the chapter on anger, you may want to go to the end of this chapter and take a brief test to see where you rate on the anger scale. And then read the chapter to give yourself ways to adjust when dealing with anger, if needed.

I had a different beginning for this chapter until June 12, 2016, when a terrorist--a madman--killed 49 people and injured many more in a mass shooting in Orlando, Florida. In the aftermath, many were rushing to try to figure out the reason it happened. TIME magazine interviewed the murderer's first wife: Once after he had attacked her, she asked why. He claimed he was *angry* that she hadn't finished the laundry. He later revealed that he'd had a fight with his father. *"Omar was always trying to impress him and be the perfect son,"* she said. His father suggested that his terrorist son was probably *angered* by gay men after seeing two men kissing in Miami a few weeks earlier. The shooting took place at a gay bar, a place Omar allegedly had frequented in the past.(TIME. June 27, 2016)

We will never know the exact reasons for this killer's massacre of 49 people and the maiming of 53 others; law enforcers killed him at the scene. However, it's an easy guess that anger was involved, and he was out of control because of other mental problems.

We all get angry, and clearly not to the extent of that murderer, but can we hold our tempers in check when dealing with the people in our lives? It can be challenging when certain people irritate us. If we want to stay in control in our relationships, we can use simple anger management tips found in this chapter—from taking a timeout to using "I" statements.

Anger: Does your blood pressure go UP when you're trying so hard to be calm with your toddler or teen, co-worker or pet? Do you get angry at your partner when she is late—again? Or he comes home smelling like alcohol from a few drinks with the guys? Do you have fights with your live-in adult son or daughter who moved back home to save money? Then, there's outside the home areas: Do you get angry at a store clerk who is being rude, or at stores whose prices go up while your salary remains the same? Or your job keeps getting harder with no extra pay?

Do you get angry when you're in an argument with your spouse, and it's beginning to escalate? Or you are at the school to talk to the principal about your daughter's outfit, which you and she believe follows the dress code, but the school principal clearly does not? Or your supervisor is assessing your work, and you are unhappy with the rating and want to quit that job and tell her to *shove it*?

Anger is a normal and even healthy emotion, but you may need ways to handle it so you can maintain your relationships. If you can't control your anger, then your health and relationships will probably be affected. I have created an Anger Rating Scale to rate your anger level. If you haven't already, please see Worksheet 7A at the end of this chapter and in the Worksheet Section.

PENN'S ANGER CONTROL DOS & DON'TS:

~**DO** decide if you are going to let someone else's words or actions control your behavior. Instead of counting to ten like some of the experts tell you to do, say to yourself, "YES, I am controlling my actions!" And for a calming, positive result, you can say to yourself, "YES, I feel calm. I feel relaxed. I feel in control. I am calm. I am relaxed. I am in control."

~**DO** know it's *your choice* to show your anger in each situation.

~**DO** know it's *your choice* to turn and walk away. Then, if you need to, do it. Walk away and out to get some distance and to cool off.

~**DO** know it's *your choice* to put your relaxation skills to work. Practice deep-breathing exercises; or, imagine a beautiful, quiet place where you'd like to be.

~**DO**, when you're away from the anger source, focus on resolving the issue. If your child's cluttered room makes you angry, close the door and think of ways you can reward the child when he or she cleans it. Are your friends late again for your weekly get-together? Ask them if they'd like to schedule it for later and less often.

~**DO** talk it out when the anger's not there. If it flares up again, remember DOs & DON'Ts. Patiently, find some common ground with which you can work together to clear it up. Help the other person see that you want this to work.

~**DO**, when you're ready to discuss the issues, use "I" statements to avoid criticizing. Use the "I" statements to describe the problems, and be specific. Example: "I'm upset that you sat in the den watching television while I prepared dinner and you didn't offer to help." Don't say: "You never help out." Be polite and respectful.

~**DO** use humor if you're comfortable with it. It can work in many situations; not so good in others. It can give the message that you aren't angry any longer. When using humor, it's safest to make fun of yourself; not the other person.

~**DO**, after the episode is over, ask yourself what made you angry, and what you can do in the future to *nip it in the bud*. Can you use statements to the person to diffuse their anger or hurt feelings? Maybe try: "I understand why you're angry with me." Or, "I don't blame you if you don't want to forgive me."

~**DO** know when to seek professional help. Learning to control anger can be difficult for some. If you or someone in your family seems out of control, causing you or them to do things you'll both regret, it may be time to get outside help. Don't hesitate to seek treatment.

~**DO** say to yourself, "I won this one by staying calm."

~**DO** know you can apologize. You don't lose by apologizing; you and the other person both win. In some cases, this works to diffuse the situation.

~**DON'T** count to ten. Substitute a more positive way to calm yourself by saying *"YES, I do control my actions."* And, *"YES, I feel calm. I feel relaxed. I feel in control....I am calm. I am relaxed. I am in control."*

~**DON'T** defend yourself. Being the victim is a role (or hole) so easy to fall into. When we defend ourselves, we are treating the other person as the enemy.

~**DON'T** give the other person the control to get you angry. When you do that, they win.

~**DON'T** be afraid. If I'm scared of you, I'm putting you in the strong position, and I lose.

~**DON'T** attack. If we attack each other, we act like enemies. It takes two people to fight. If you attack me, it only becomes a fight if I attack back.

~**DON'T** hold a grudge. Learn ways to let it go as soon as you can; preferably sooner than later. If you let it go, a weight will be lifted from both of you.

I've summarized the pointers, *Penn's Anger Control DOs and DON'Ts*, and you can copy it as a poster. Please see it near the end of this chapter and in the Posters Section.

"Violence is not inevitable, it is learned. And it can be unlearned," said Esta Soler, a founder of Futures Without Violence. Watch the full @TEDTalks from Esta Soler: *http://bit.ly/1JvVQFw*.

Violence in American homes is common. *Futures Without Violence* reports on the violence that children and parents experience in their home. Please go to the website for statistics; they are amazing! *futureswithoutviolence.org*

Because many abused women have children, often they will try to protect them with their lives, going to incredible lengths to shield them from the abusers. Adult counseling clients have told me of the fears they had growing up in a violent home and of the terrifying and traumatic experiences that have affected every aspect of their life and have continued to affect them as adults.

Many children who live with violence in their homes have the symptoms of post-traumatic stress disorder (PTSD), just like adults who suffer from war involvement and other disasters. Some of the behaviors seen in children are nightmares, bedwetting, allergies, asthma, stomachaches, headaches, etc. These symptoms continue into adulthood if not treated properly.

When the children become adults, they are also at risk of having other health problems including the ones they had as a child. Others include substance abuse, alcoholism, tobacco use, obesity, depression, and other more serious illnesses like cancer and heart disease.

When women who experience prenatal physical domestic violence have their babies, the infants are at risk of having behaviors such as sleep and feeding disorders, aggression, anxiety, or hyperactivity.

Psychotherapy can help these parents and children. It can increase the quality of parenting and increase positive outcomes for children. Some parents may be motivated to stop using violence if they understand the devastating effects on their children.

I wrote an essay when I was counseling children and parents who deal with or have dealt with out-of-control anger in their lives. I have included this article in the nonfiction section of my previously published book: *Landscapes of a Mind.* I've added two more anger case studies to the version in this book at the beginning to show angry parents who did not receive anger-management counseling and, also later in the article, a statement about a mass killer.

FROM HOT-HEAD TO COOL CAT
(names are changed)

A young father in Florida killed his eight-year-old daughter in the 1990s by beating and kicking her to death. Many people in this beautiful child's life saw signs of abuse: blackened eyes, bruises, and her limping from the pain of possibly dislocated bones. Some people reported what they saw: school teachers, medical staff, and family friends; but the child protection staff of the State of Florida allegedly took no action to protect the child. The father told reporters that he had asked for help from these same state workers in dealing with his anger toward the child, but, if he asked for help, none was given.

Searchers found her body where the father buried her in a shallow grave in a national forest. He is now serving a life sentence in prison for the murder of his daughter.

Judy, a young, single mother was convicted and sentenced to prison for many years, with additional years of probation for the long-time, severe physical and emotional abuse of her son, Scotty, who was six years old when the abuse started and 12 years old when it was discovered. When I counseled with him, he lived with a foster family and wanted to be adopted by them. He had learned from them how a "real mother and father" treat their children. His biological father was absent from his life.

In an interview at the county jail before she went to state prison, Judy told this writer that she would get angry at Scotty and abuse him, and when she would see the blood and bruises, she would say to herself that she'd never harm him again. But, she admittedly never asked for help, so, without intervention, she continued to hurt him. Judy home-schooled him so that no one would see his bruises and scars. When he would make mistakes in his school work, she would physically punish him. Once she bent his finger back until it broke when he did not memorize a bible verse.

As a nurse, she would take her son to jobs tending to the homebound elderly. The extended family noticed how close she kept him by her side when they would visit, not allowing him to play with his young cousins, but they never intervened.

In addition to the many scars he will carry on his body, there were injuries on his head where hair will no longer grow due to his mother's blows from her high-heel shoe. After she had lost her home, she moved in with her mother and, at night; she would bind Scotty's arms, tape his mouth, and put him in the closet while she slept so he could not tell his grandmother what was happening to him. Other times, she would tie him to the bed and blindfold him so he couldn't roam around the house or escape to report what was happening to him. When discovered, he had rope burns on both wrists and stated that his hands are now numb from being tied up for extended periods of time over the years.

When discovered by the police and child welfare workers, Scotty was wearing diapers due to accidentally soiling and wetting his clothes. He told me he was not given food for five days at a time as punishment. In anger, she once smashed his face onto a kitchen counter which broke his two front teeth. When she lost her temper, she would punch him in the eye with her fist, gouge his eyes with her fingernails, claw his face and chest, and pinch him on the face. Once, she stabbed him in the chest with scissors, then taped it together rather than take him to the hospital for stitches. He now has a two-inch scar with keloids on his chest. "When my mother would discover I had stained my clothes, she would put me in scalding hot water in the shower." Once removed from her, he reported that he never had another accident.

He received weekly in-home or in-school psychotherapy. Scotty, who was an attractive young man and extremely outgoing, was doing well in the foster home and making good grades in school when I last saw him. He hopes he can see his mother when she leaves prison. He will be an adult then and can make that decision.

Mary, a 29-year-old single mother, lives in Florida with her three children, Jenny, Sam, and Nellie. Neighbors recently reported her to the state agency that investigates child abuse because she was frequently seen and heard hitting Jenny, age eight, and Sam, age six. She often left two-year-old Nellie alone in the apartment with the two older children when the sitter didn't arrive in time for her to get to her job as a salesperson in a department store. She has no family in the central Florida town where she has lived for the past few years since she left her abusive husband.

Mary was surprised that anyone would report her for abuse, saying she spanked her children to make them mind her; that she wasn't abusing them, but teaching them to be good kids. She did not want to acknowledge that her son had hit the two-year-old, and often had fights with his older sister.

Mary considered herself to be a good mother, supporting her children and taking care of them with no help from their father, her extended family, or the welfare department. She left her husband when she realized he would not change—he would hit her and the children and then beg her to forgive him, time after time. Finally, Mary left. She wonders how she had the strength to go, after living with the abuse for so long.

Before parents can teach their children about anger control, they have to learn for themselves the facts about the emotion that has caused so much grief and pain. Mary agreed to attend parenting and anger-management classes and later said she never knew there was another way to discipline her children other than the way she learned as a child. "I thought that I had to hit them to make them mind me; that's how my mom did it. I remember getting the belt on my back when I would 'sass' her. I hit my kids many times when I was angry, and I'd tell them that it hurt me more than it hurt them. Now, I'm learning how to control my anger, and I don't hit them anymore."

In Mary's classes, she learned some basic facts about anger: It's an integral part of a person; if denied or repressed, it will emerge in destructive ways, often unexpected. We must recognize its signals, know when we are feeling it, and try to locate its origins. To do that, we have to stop ourselves immediately from acting on the feeling and try to figure out where it's coming from.

This action takes a lot of practice, but we can learn to take time out to sort out the feeling and the way we plan to express it. There are several ways we first expressed our anger which we learned from watching others when they are angry. We adapt to these styles because we learned this is how our parents or guardians expressed anger.

Some ways we express anger:

Hiding Anger. *Sometimes, we hide our anger when we don't want to or are afraid to confront directly the person or situation that is provoking the wrath. However, it can be expressed in other forms: sarcasm, unintentionally forgetting to do something for someone, holding back love, or avoiding the person or situation in the future. Hidden anger is hard to recognize because the people who hide it deny that they are angry, even when confronted. Hidden anger results in many physical and mental illnesses such as ulcers, migraine headaches, obesity, and depression.*

Inflating Anger. *This is much easier to identify than hidden. Inflators usually begin their sentences with You; they blame others for their problems, they shame their partner and children and try to make them feel guilty, and they attack physically. People who inflate their anger may get their way, but only for a short time. Our opponents may give in to avoid our fury, but they will probably get back at us somehow, even in a disguised manner.*

Inner-directing Anger. *We need to be aware of the dangers of inner-directed anger which we direct at ourselves and can cause depression.*

Displacing Anger. *This is aimed at an inappropriate target. An example of displaced anger: a man goes home and yells at his family or kicks the dog after his boss yelled at him at work. While displaced anger may make you angrier which is self-defeating, you now have the anger recipient upset at you.*

Handling Anger. *This is a productive style because we clearly and appropriately express to the provoking person that we are angry at him or her. Individuals who express their anger directly get their message across, communicate better and feel as though they have made contact in a personal manner. The more aware we become of how we express our anger, the more* control we have over dealing with it. Handling anger is a result of telling ourselves we are in control, remaining calm and walking away if necessary.

Now that you have some tools to help you with anger, you can begin immediately to practice anger control, if needed; and should do so, starting right now. Why wait? The next time you feel the emotion, you can "get physical"—take a long fast walk, go for a bike ride, walk on a treadmill, scrub floors or walls, or rip up old papers or magazines.

Some other ways that are less physical can also be effective: write about your anger, either in a journal or letters you tear up. Talking with a friend or therapist will help you understand the particular cause of your anger, and crying releases the frustrations. Deep breathing and meditation can help muscles to relax and can resolve the physical component of your anger.

Note: Don't spread the cause of your anger around on social media—it can create a problem if it gets to the wrong person.

Another mother and son I worked with, Karen and her eight-year-old son, Tim, came to me because Tim stayed in trouble with the neighborhood children and their parents because of his temper; he just could not keep his cool when he was playing with them. Karen believed that he had inherited these strong feelings from his father, but she also blamed herself because of her behavior toward the child. During the period following her divorce, Karen was under much stress because of financial problems and the uncertainty of her and her son's future, and she seemed to take it out on Tim. With professional help, she learned better ways to control her behavior and new ways to help her son.

Karen learned that modeling the correct way to express emotions will help both her and Tim. She also found there are techniques and tools specially designed to help children learn the best way to act.

ChildsWork/ChildsPlay is a catalog with items which addresses the behavioral, social, and emotional needs of children, and can to be used by both parents and counselors. These are books, games, and workbooks which use activities to help children and teens learn nonaggressive alternatives to conflict. I've used these, and they are excellent. The free catalog can be ordered online at their website: ChildsWork.com, or call: 1-800-962-1141.

Karen recently completed her counseling. On the last day with the *therapist, she reported that Tim said he wishes everybody knew how to show and tell others how they feel in a way that doesn't get them into trouble. Both Karen and Tim have found new ways to express themselves when they have stress. They now feel good about themselves and the way they relate to each other and other people in their lives, and Tim went from being a Hot Head to a Cool Dude.*

And, remember Mary, mother of three young children, our first success story after she was in her parenting and anger-management classes? Now she's helping to teach those classes, and brags about helping young parents learn new and better ways to discipline their children, and, most of all, to control their feelings before they get out-of-hand.

**"If you are patient in one moment of anger,
you will escape a hundred days of sorrow."**
Chinese Proverb

To stay calm on the road (other times, too):

"Try this breathing exercise-Inhale through your nose
for five seconds, hold for five seconds, then exhale for five
seconds. Repeat for two minutes or until you feel calm."
– R. Douglas Fields, neuroscientist and author

POSTER
ANGER CONTROL
Penn's DOs and DON'Ts:

~DO decide if you will let others control your behavior.

~DO know you choose to show anger.

~DO know you choose to turn away.

~DO know you choose to relax.

~DO talk it out when the anger is gone.

~DO avoid criticizing.

~DO use humor.

~DO know you can apologize.

~DO say, "I won by staying calm."

~DON'T count to ten; use a positive statement, e.g., *I am calm, I am relaxed…*

~DON'T FORGET-do one thing at a time.

Print and post where you and others will see it.

CHECKLIST & CONTRACT

I WILL COMPLETE THIS CHECKLIST & CONTRACT FOR EACH BEHAVIOR I WORK ON.

____ I am motivated to change/improve my behavior:
Name Behavior: Managing My Anger

____ I begin by working to improve one behavior at a time.

____ I will complete this checklist for my behavior improvement.

____ I will sign a contract and place it where I can see it often.

____ I will work with another person to improve this behavior.

____ I will keep a journal about my progress and feelings.

____ I will read Chapters 1 & 2.

____ I will complete the worksheets for Chapters 1 & 2.

____ I will read the chapter of the behavior I want to improve.

____ I will complete the worksheet(s) relevant to the chapter.

CONTRACT

As of today, I choose to improve my life,
one behavior at a time, by **Managing My Anger.**

Name_____ Date_____

Print and Post

WORKSHEET 7A

ANGER RATING SCALE

Read the statements, and then write the appropriate number by it to indicate how you feel most of the time, or for the past weeks.

Never=1   **Rarely=2**   **Sometimes=3**
Often=4   **Most of the time=5**

I hold on to angry feelings. _____

I get angry with my family. _____

I am known as a hot-headed person. _____

I get angry at other drivers when I am driving. _____

I feel anger when I am not praised for doing good work. _____

I get angry with co-workers and salespeople. _____

I say nasty things when I am angry. _____

I feel anger when I am falsely accused. _____

When I get frustrated, I feel like hitting someone. _____

I show my temper by yelling at others. _____

ADD YOUR NUMBERS _____

Scoring is on the next page.

SCORING:

If you scored below 29, you are among the least angry people.

If you scored 30-39, your anger level is about average.

If you scored 40 or more, your anger level is higher than most people.

WORKSHEET 7B

Manage Your Anger

Use 7 Easy-to-Follow Anger Management Tips.
Choose one behavior at a time until it becomes a habit.

When you're angry, do this:

Daily Tasks   Times Tried

1-Think before you speak;
once you're calm,
express your anger---

2-Stick with 'I' statements---

3-Get some exercise---

4-Take a timeout when angry---

5-Identify possible solutions---

6-Use humor to release tension---

7-Practice relaxation skills---

> ***If you believe you need more help controlling your anger other than the suggestions included in this chapter, please contact a mental health provider, or call* 1-800-553-4539 or 1-888-269-4389.**

Sharon W. Penn 2017 Change 1 Behavior, Improve Your Life.
Email me: sharonwpenn@gmail.com

Chapter 8

Behavior Change:
Enhance Your Personal Relationship

The most important thing to remember about intimate relationships is to cherish and nurture that important person in your life.

Does it sometimes appear that your partner gives his attention to co-workers or old buddies more than he gives attention to you and your children? Or, do you seem to nurture your children more than you do your partner? Yes, of course, you do, some mothers tell me. Some men have expressed that when the children come along, the wife forgets about him, and he feels neglected. She might say that of course her focus is on the young children and he should "get over it," but some men think they deserve as much attention as the children; and many wives know that. So, cherish and nurture him, and the children will see that their dad is important, too—a valuable lesson for them. The same for the dad to cherish their mom. And they will both cherish and nurture the children.

This chapter will be about couples in intimate relationships. Another chapter will talk about friendships with other people. Parent/child relationships are covered in many other excellent books. See a bibliography in Chapter 8 Notes.

Partner Relationships-Since this chapter will address spouses and other intimate adult live-ins, I want to be able to use an umbrella term for all of them. One friend calls her guy The Sweetheart when she writes about him on Facebook.

And I found an article on the internet called: 47 Better Ways to Refer to Your Significant Other Than 'Boyfriend' or 'Girlfriend.' My favorite there was 'the old balls and chain.' The writer of the blog, Molly Fitzgerald, said she is utterly mystified as to why her boyfriend doesn't think her calling him this is nearly as hilarious as she does. Hmmm. I think I'll stick with partner or mate; that can cover many different intimate relationships.

When people are in these types of relationships—whether legal marriages, common-law marriages, long-term relationships, newer live-ins, or steady dating—they are primarily about the emotional responsiveness we call love; about a fundamental human attachment. Dr. Susan Johnson, a California therapist, says "these intimacy bonds reflect deep primal survival needs for secure, intimate connection to irreplaceable others."

Much research has been done to study important attachment relationships, and we now know how important attachments are throughout life for physical and mental well-being. Studies show that those closest to us have a direct impact on our ability to regulate our physiological as well as our emotional processes.

Most of us need someone (our person) to see and hear us— someone to be there for us when we are at our most vulnerable. In healthy, secure relationships, we get that from our mates.

Dr. John Gottman has been studying couples for more than 20 years; his method is unique. Couples are invited to his "Love Lab," in Seattle, Washington, where they are miked-up, wired for sensors that record heart rate and other physiological signs, recorded on video camera and watched from behind a two-way mirror.

Dr. Gottman gives the couples some privacy; the bathroom isn't recorded, and the cameras only roll between 9 AM and 9 PM. But Dr. Gottman isn't interested in what happens in the bedroom; he believes he can predict with over 90% accuracy whether your relationship will last or fail just by watching you argue for 5 minutes.

Couples argue; sometimes a lot and sometimes a little. Dr. Gottman says that arguing makes little or no difference to your overall happiness and likelihood of staying together. It's the *way* you argue that predicts how things will work out.

Two more quotes of Dr. Gottman relevant to this chapter on personal relationships:

> "A smile, a head nod, even just grunting to show you're listening to your partner—those are all positive."

> "In any interaction, we have the opportunity to connect with our partner or to turn away. If we consistently turn away, then over time the foundation of the marriage [relationship] can slowly erode."

You can learn more about Dr. Gottman in his many books about relationships. He has tests to rate your relationship and ways to better the relationship, if it needs it. See Chapter 8 Notes.

I wrote this article about learning to argue maturely for my counseling clients. Please let me know if it's helpful in your relationships.

LEARN TO ARGUE MATURELY

"Do nothing from selfishness or empty conceit, but with humility of mind let each of you regard one another as more important than himself; do not merely look out for your own personal interests, but also for the interests of others."
(Philippians 2:3-4: King James Bible)

You are going to have an argument with someone, sometime, somewhere. Learning to communicate with others during times of distress and anger, and to argue maturely requires time and effort. Learning how to argue can take some time to find a balance.

First of all, when we are teens or young adults, we each go into a relationship with our ways of arguing based on what we learned as a child. Some people learned as children that if they cried loud enough and whined long enough, they would eventually get their way. Others learned sulking and pouting could get them what they wanted.

It's hard to shake off old habits of behavior and start new ones. (We see this in Chapter 2—"Why It's Hard to Change a Habit...".) Some people say they have to stop themselves in their tracks to get out of their "upset child" mode and then to communicate in a mature way.

You may want to try these *TIPS TO HELP YOU ARGUE MORE SUSSESSFULLY*:

*- **LISTEN** to the other person's point of view, taking into consideration his/her past experiences that are very different from yours. Make sure you acknowledge their point of view; you don't have to agree with what they are saying, but you do need to show you've gotten the message. An example: "I think I can see how you might feel." Then, they can tell you if you've gotten it right. The main thing is that you are paying attention, so they feel they're being heard.*

Both (or all) of you will have to transition from intense conflict to useful communication to resolve the argument. Begin by listening and understanding one another. Actively listen and understand what the other is saying. In turn, this slows down the process and allows each person to feel heard and understood. In counseling, I've used an object that the speaker holds when they are talking which reminds the listener to wait to speak until they are holding the object. It can be anything (other than a sharp object). I used a small squeeze ball which they passed between or among themselves.

*- **YOU can ask for time to think about what's being said**. You can say that you respect what they have to say and deserve a proper answer. Say that you don't want to answer instantly, and you want to come back to discuss it later. Set a time, if possible.*

Allowing space for both or all of you to cool down will have a positive outcome in the end. It's hard to think clearly when you're stressed, so physically distancing yourself can help your emotions to relax. Don't leave until you've explained that you need some space and want to resume the discussion at some later time.

*- **People deal with conflict differently** because everyone, male or female, has different methods that work successfully for them. For example, some*

women may want to vent, as talking increases oxytocin, the feel-good chemical. If being heard is all a woman wants, then she may want to preface the conversation that she just wants her listener to be all ears and try to understand her point of view.

Men want to either fight or take flight when they are challenged, or they are fixers that want to find solutions.

*~ **Don't get side-tracked**. Take one thing at a time, and keep to the point. It's not about getting the other person to agree with you but it's about them hearing your perspective.*

*~ **Don't try to talk about too many things at one time**. Pick one and stick with it.*

*~ **Try techniques** like "brainstorming" and "pros vs. cons" lists to find a solution.*

*~ **Forgiveness** has to take place for the process to be complete. Resentment or anger can continue after the conflict has ended if there have been heated words, so try to identify your contribution to the problem and offer your apologies, if needed. If the dispute is not resolved, and one or both of you are exhausted from the strain of arguing, it might be time to find someone like a counselor or a pastor to intercede and help bring about a resolution.*

***You will always have to modify and adapt to the different people you interact with in your life**. You've probably found that out already. They will all come with different personalities and habits. So to have tools available to you when an argument occurs puts you in a positive position to help the relationship. When you are at a point of losing it, remember that these tools can save the day.*

Please see the POSTER to ARGUE MATURELY Penn's DOs and DON'Ts at the end of the chapter.

Also, please see the POSTER for RELATIONSHIPS Penn's Dos and DON'Ts following ARGUE MATURELY.

Periodic Performance Review-One of the newest ideas in counseling for couples is for therapists to recommend partners complete regular performance reviews; they say couples typically wait too long to go to therapy for help.

The worksheet for this chapter is a self-rating scale I designed for couples who feel their relationship needs work. It's a good place to start. See Worksheet 8 at the end of this chapter. Both partners complete it and then share with each other to see where they agree or differ. They may then decide to get guidance from a therapist, or they may believe they can work out their issues on their own. Please see at the end of this chapter and in the Worksheet Section.

POSTER
ARGUE MATURELY
Penn's DOs and DON'Ts:

~DO LISTEN. Try to see the other point of view.

~DO ASK FOR TIME to think about what's being said.

~DO KNOW PEOPLE DEAL with CONFLICT DIFFERENTLY.

~DO FIND a "WIN-WIN" SOLUTION.

~DON'T GET SIDE-TRACKED. Take one thing at a time, and keep to the point.

~DON'T TALK ABOUT TOO MANY THINGS AT ONCE. Pick one and stick with it.

~DO KNOW FORGIVENESS HAS TO TAKE PLACE for the process to be complete.

~DON'T FORGET. Do only one thing at a time. Pick one and do it now.

Print and post where you and others will see it.

POSTER
RELATIONSHIPS
PENN'S DOs and DON'Ts:

-DO CHERISH and NOURISH THE IMPORTANT PEOPLE IN YOUR LIFE.

-DO COMPLIMENT THEM WITH SPECIFICS.

-DO NOTICE THEM OFTEN--SEE & HEAR.

-DO TELL THEM OFTEN HOW IMPORTANT THEY ARE TO YOU.

-DO HAVE 'SIT-DOWN' REVIEWS TOGETHER.

-DON'T TURN AWAY.

-DON'T FORGET-do only one thing at a time.

Print and post where you and others will see it.

CHECKLIST & CONTRACT

I WILL COMPLETE THIS CHECKLIST & CONTRACT
FOR EACH BEHAVIOR I WORK ON.

____ I am motivated to change/improve my behavior:
Name Behavior: **Enhance My Relationship.**

____ I will begin by working to improve one behavior at a time.

____ I will complete this checklist for each behavior.

____ I will sign a contract and place it where I can see it often.

____ I will work with another person to improve this behavior.

____ I will keep a journal about my progress and feeling.

____ I will read Chapters 1 & 2.

____ I will complete the worksheets for Chapters 1 & 2.

____ I will read the chapter of the behavior I want to improve.

____ I will complete the worksheet(s) relevant to this chapter.

CONTRACT

As of today, I choose to improve my life, one behavior
at a time, by **Enhancing My RELATIONSHIP.**

Name_____ Date_____

Print and Post

WORKSHEET 8

RELATIONSHIP REVIEW FOR COUPLES

Both partners complete the rating individually and then share with each other to see where they agree or differ. They may then decide to get guidance from a therapist, or they may believe they can work out their issues on their own.

1- Describe the relationship with your partner.
Superb__ Good__ Fair__ Poor__ Very Poor__
Comments_____

2- What attracted you the most to your partner? (Choose 3)
Sex__ Physical__ Intelligent__ Communicates well__ Personality__
Financial__ Influence of family/friends__
Similar backgrounds/interests__
Other_____

3- If choosing a partner now, what would attract you the most? (Choose 3)
Sex__ Physical__ Intelligent__ Financial__ Communicates well__
Personality__ Influence of family/friends__
Similar backgrounds/interests__
Other_____

4- Describe positive feelings you have with this partner. (Choose as many as you want) Contented__ Loved__ Appreciated__ Satisfied__ Able to share feelings__ Equals__ Self-confident__ Calm__ Proud__ Sexually compatible__ Independent__
Other_____

5~ Describe negative feelings you have with this partner. (Choose as many as you want)

Unloved__ Tied down__ Isolated__ Overwhelmed__ Trapped__
Unappreciated__ Afraid__ Dissatisfied__ Feel controlled__
Nervous__ Depressed__ Sexually frustrated__
Lonely__ Unable to share feelings__ None__
Other_____

6~ How do you divide responsibilities between you two?
I have all__ I have the most__ Divided fairly__
Partner has the most__ Partner has all__

7~ Conflicts with this partner. (Choose as many as you want)
Personal habits__ Infidelity__ Being ignored__ Financial__
Sex together__ Communication__ Children__ Family__
My job__ Partner's job__ Religion__ Politics__ Personal interests__
Alcohol/Drugs__ Other_____

8~ How do you deal with stress? (Choose as many as you want)
Pray__ Meditate__ Yoga__ Exercise__ Cry__
Talk with partner__ Talk with friend__ Alcohol__
Drugs__ Prescribed tranquilizers__ Watch TV__
Social Media__ Express aggression__ Hobbies__
Other_____

9~ In the past few months have you often had? Anger__
Depression__ Headaches__ Insomnia__ Irritability__ Anxiety__
Uninterested in sex__ Cry easily__ Stomach issues__
Feeling I can't go on__ Lonely__
Gaining or losing weight__ Tiring easily__
Guilty feeling__ Unable to concentrate__ Tense__ Worried__
Other_____

10- What big change could your partner make to have this relationship work better? _____

_____

11- What big changes could you make to have this relationship work better? _____

_____

12-Please rate your life overall.
Splendid __ Good __ Fair__ Poor__ Very Poor__
Comments_____

Any additional comments?

Sharon W. Penn 2017 Change 1 Behavior, Improve Your Life.
Email me: sharonwpenn@gmail.com

Chapter 9

Behavior Change:
Focus On Healthy Living:
Diet, Exercise, Sleep

Please start this chapter by completing Worksheet 9 at the end of the chapter, which gives you an idea of ways you can improve your health—one behavior at a time.

There is a ton of information on these three behaviors, both on the internet and in books, so here are some helpful TIPS. Please send me tips that work for you, if you don't find them here.
Email me: *sharonwpenn@gmail.com*

DIET

So many diets to consider: Mediterranean, DASH, Paleo, Vegan, Atkins, South Beach and many more. The diets listed here have a lot in common. They recommend more vegetables than the average American eats, more fruits, fewer refined grains, and fewer sugars and sugary drinks. These are not just for weight loss, but also a guide for a healthier way of life.

Gaples Institute for Integrative Cardiology—a nonprofit that balances natural strategies with conventional medicine—has an excellent blog and a newsletter with updated information on foods and nutrition.

They suggest that eating vegetables and fruits will leave less room for junk food. The fiber in vegetables and fruits is very filling, leaving less of an appetite for low-quality food. Avoiding refined grains and sugary beverages is an easy way to eliminate the vast majority of junk food. Eating lots of vegetables and fruits may be an effective damage control plan; for example, high blood pressure relevant to excess sodium intake (often from junk food) may be offset by increased intake of potassium (concentrated in fruit). Note: Diabetics need to be mindful of sugars in fruits.

I am on their mailing list for their updates, and you can be, too. Go to: *www.gaplesinstitute.org/update-me.* Gaples Institute for Integrative Cardiology invites you to sign up for the newsletter and to enjoy their blog while there. In a recent blog, for example, they inform us that almonds are designated a *"Gaples Staple"* because they rank exceptionally high in health, taste, and affordability.

A study explains why people who eat nuts regularly (almonds and walnuts are best studied) have a significantly lower risk of heart disease. One large study showed a 37% reduced risk of heart disease with four servings of nuts a week.

Some people are concerned about weight gain from nuts because of their high caloric density--200 calories for a handful of nuts. Interestingly enough, most studies don't show a weight gain with nuts; many even show a tendency toward weight loss!

Part of the explanation is nuts are not completely digested. Another theory (not yet confirmed) is that nuts act as a probiotic, helping to nurture healthy bacteria in the gut that contributes to maintaining a normal weight. Regardless, the best practice, as shown in the first study mentioned, is to substitute nuts for other less healthy snacks you might be eating. Nuts are ideal for keeping in a pocket or purse during the day for snacking on the run. Use a small container or plastic sandwich bag to put in a few nuts from a larger bag for daily transporting.

Losing Weight. Many of us know the key to weight loss is making changes in our eating patterns. Many diet experts suggest we trim some calories each day by eating smaller portions, eating more fruits and vegetables, and by increasing activity, either by exercise or walking more. You can do this—one food, one behavior at a time.

Intermittent Fasting, which Dr. Joseph Mercola calls *effortless eating,* is a way to lose weight; and there are many ways to program your fasting. Some of them are: *Eat Stop Eat, The Warrior Diet, Fat Loss Forever, and Alternate-Day Fasting,* which is *effortless eating* and my favorite. This one is easy: eat lightly one day (about 500 calories), then the next day, eat normal (about 2200 calories or less). You can research them all online. Dr. Mercola's book is *Effortless Healing* (2015).

If you want to lose weight and use a support group, try Weight Watchers. Oprah Winfrey, an American media proprietor, talk show host, actress, producer, and philanthropist, long-time focused on weight loss, has recently aligned with them. They have a stellar reputation for helping people lose weight and keep it off (maintenance). *www. weightwatchers.com.* As I've written in another chapter, having a support group—even just one other person—can help keep you focused on your goal, whatever it is.

Listed here, alphabetically by author, are some popular diet books offering many ideas and tips on how to make small and gradual behavior changes. Check some out at the library, or buy at bookstores or Amazon Books.

Amsterdam, Elana. *Paleo Cooking from Elana's Pantry: Gluten-free, Grain-free, Dairy-free Recipes.* N.Y. Ten Speed Press. 2013. Here are simple paleo recipes that emphasize protein and produce, from breakfasts to entrees to treats. The Paleo diet emphasizes meat and seafood, vegetables, fruits, and nuts. Nearly 100 recipes feature the Paleo suggestions of lean proteins and simple vegetable dishes, plus wholesome sweet treats--all free from grains, gluten, and dairy, and made with natural sweeteners.

Cruise, Jorge. *Inches Off! Your Tummy: The Super-Simple 5-Minute Plan to Firm Up...*N.Y. Rodale. 2013. Jorge Cruise's new book presents one piece of advice in his new fitness and weight-loss series: Work smarter, not harder. *In Inches Off! Your Tummy,* Jorge unveils the most efficient exercise formula to optimize belly fat burn. He also shows us how to avoid the hidden sugars in foods that signal our bodies to store fat. He says we will have visible results in six days, exercising just five minutes per day. Jorge Cruise has over six million books in print and is one of the most successful fitness and diet authors around.

Fletcher, Anne. *Thin for Life*. N.Y. Houghton Mifflin, 2003. The author interviewed hundreds of successful "winners" who have lost weight and kept it off to come up with ten keys to successful weight loss.

Guttersen. Connie. N.Y. (Meredith Books, 2005 *The Sonoma Diet*. Here is a diet book that allows calories for wine and lots of wonderfully healthy food. It has a sensible diet plan similar to a Mediterranean approach with lots of healthy foods.

Lillien, Lisa. *The Hungry Girl Diet Cookbook: Healthy Recipes for Mix-n-Match Meals & Snacks*. N.Y. St. Martin's Griffin. 2015. In the New York Times bestseller *The Hungry Girl Diet*, Lisa Lillien presented a diet plan utilizing her philosophy and recipes. She now has a companion cookbook, which features 200 all-new recipes that work with the groundbreaking diet plan! You may want both books.

Spiker, Ted. *Down Size: 12 Truths for Turning Pants-Splitting Frustration Into Pants-Fitting Success*. N.Y. Hudson Street Press. 2014. Ted takes a humorous approach as he explores weight loss through his own struggles as a pear-shaped man. He has research about food, exercise, and the psychology of losing weight. He reveals twelve truths about successful weight loss, in areas such as temptation, frustration, nutrition, and inspiration.

Weight Watchers. This successful company has a variety of books and programs, and now Oprah! The programs direct dieters to get connected at meetings (in person or online) for motivation, support, and sustainability of lifestyle changes.

EXERCISE

A support group can be a key benefit to helping you stay with an exercise program, whether it's gardening, walking, running, biking, swimming, yoga, or working out at the gym or at home. There are chair exercises that work for the elderly, office workers, and beginners. There are numerous ways to get a workout and starting slowly is important.

Sometimes it's difficult to coordinate with another person when your schedules conflict or you live long distances apart. One of our research teams used the telephone as two individuals kept in touch to "report in" about their daily walking, choosing a convenient time for them to alternate calling each other. Using email or texting can also work well, and calling while exercising, whether walking, using the treadmill, or biking "fill two needs with one deed," (that is, if you remain mindful of your surroundings).

A few years ago, another psychotherapist, Dr. Margaret Click, and I led a group which we called Creative Weight Control (CWC). Because we all had jobs, we met alternate weeks to report on our food plan and exercise schedule, and to discuss our experiences. We used hypnosis in the meetings, an audio tape for hypnosis by Dr. Click for use at home, and numerous handouts on exercise and recipes as aids. The group only lasted for a few months due to work conflicts, and I've been thinking about what we learned during our time together.

This concept of CWC could be used by two or more people, using relaxation, meditation, or yoga instead of hypnosis. They could use accountability of their exercise, yoga, and weigh-in to report results, and if money is collected it could be kept in an account to be used as a reward for trips when an agreed-upon event is planned.

SLEEP

We need sleep to maintain good health and to look, feel, and perform each day at our maximum best. But, many of us--almost one-third, possibly more--suffer from insomnia; some of us on a regular basis, and others just once in a while. Some studies have found that older adults mention sleep problems more often than do younger adults—generally, more than half of the responders 65 and older reported at least one sleep complaint. Women tend to have more trouble than men, especially after menopause.

Up to 90% of people with chronic medical conditions, i.e., arthritis, heartburn, and heart disease, also experience insomnia. Others believe their obesity and depression cause them not to sleep properly.

Other insomniacs say their sleep is interrupted by life stresses, like a job loss or change; death of a loved one; unresolved family problems with children, teens, or even adult children; divorce; relocation; their illness or a loved one's illness; and emotional or physical discomfort. There can be environmental factors like any noise, light, or temperatures as reasons for not being able to go to sleep or stay asleep. Some medications, like those used to treat colds and allergies, depression, high blood pressure, and asthma may interfere with sleep. Other interferences in normal sleep schedule are jet lag or switching from a day to night shift on a job. The anticipation of future happenings can cause sleeplessness— good or bad.

Many causes of chronic insomnia include depression or anxiety, chronic stress, and pain or discomfort at night. Immediate effects of insomnia are fatigue, moodiness, daytime sleepiness or naps, irritability, anger, a poor memory which leads to poor quality performance at school or work, headaches, and upset stomach. The chronic sufferers can have some health problems: weight gain, heart disease, depression, diabetes, and possibly many others—like high blood pressure, fibromyalgia, and anxiety.

Many reasons are given for sleeplessness, and many effects of insomnia are known. What works to cure the problem for one person may not work for another, but there is help for us. See if any of these tips work for you. If you know of other tips that work, please let me know. Email me: *sharonwpenn@gmail.com*

TIPS FOR INSOMNIACS:

WebMD has tips for helping you sleep at their website: *www.webmd.com/women/guide/insomnis-tips*

I'll divide the tips I'm suggesting to end your sleeplessness into four categories: **1-Your Behavior 2-Your Sleep Environment, 3-Food and Drink, and 4-Exercise.** These all can affect your sleep habits; so, please read them all, then decide the ones that affect you the most. Remember to work on only one at a time to help you to sleep better:

1-Your Behavior: Sometimes, your schedule is screwed up on weekends, so your routine is changed. Because you are at home, you may want to take a nap. Or you go to a late-night event and sleep late the next day. Studies have shown, if you have insomnia, you need to continue getting up at the same time every day to train your body to wake at a consistent time.

Naps: It seems like a good way to catch up on sleep, especially on weekends, when you have more time at home. But, napping can affect the quality of nighttime sleep, and WebMD says it's important to establish and maintain a regular sleep pattern and train oneself to associate sleep with cues like darkness and a consistent bedtime.

If these activities increase your alertness and make it difficult to fall asleep, a good book is recommended, but I say *No* to reading an exciting book that may keep you awake all night until you finish it. I'm speaking from experience. Just find a somewhat boring book that will help put you to sleep.

The insomnia experts say to limit activities in the bedroom. They say the bed is for sleeping and having sex and that's it. Sex—the hormone oxytocin, sometimes called the cuddle hormone, and which is also associated with sleep, is released during intercourse. Both men and women produce oxytocin which can be a recipe for a good night's sleep for both. Oxytocin is a powerful hormone. When we hug or kiss someone we love, oxytocin levels drive up. It also acts as a neurotransmitter in the brain. In fact, the experts say the hormone plays a huge role in pair bonding.

Other Activities--although it has become a national habit, those experts of insomnia say to avoid watching television and using computers, phones, and tablets for an hour before bed and during the night if you wake up.

Turn off your cell phone, laptop, or iPad as they are sleep deterrents. The reason is the blue wavelengths produced by your cell phone, et. al., suppress the production of melatonin, the hormone that makes you sleepy. My daughter, Jane, says she has an alarm clock with blue digits that could serve as a landing strip for incoming aircraft and that she has to cover with a cloth so it won't interfere with her sleep. Light-emitting devices engage and stimulate the mind, resulting in poorer sleep. I sometimes wear an eye cover (sleep mask or cloth) to help me sleep better.

Worrying--if you find you worry after you lie down to go to sleep, consider setting aside time earlier in the evening to review the day and to make plans for the next day. It may help to make a list of work-relevant tasks for the next day before leaving work, so you won't worry at home.

Stress--there are some relaxation-therapy methods you may want to try to relax the mind and the body before going to bed. Examples include progressive muscle relaxation with audio tapes, deep breathing techniques, imagery, meditation, and biofeedback.

Unwinding--it's smart to start unwinding early in the evening; if possible, try a few minutes of meditation. Regular meditation may help some insomniacs. We know meditation sends a signal to your sympathetic nervous system's "fight or flight" response telling it that it's all right to relax. Also, try some easy yoga poses; a few low-key yoga moves can signal to your brain that slumber is coming. Taking a warm, relaxing bath or shower before going to bed can be helpful.

Therapy--consider participating in Cognitive Behavior Therapy. It helps some people with insomnia to identify and correct inappropriate thoughts. Remember: *Therapy is educational; education can be therapeutic.*

2-Your sleep environment needs to be comfortable, and you need to have the temperature, lighting, and noise under control so you can fall asleep and stay asleep. The National Sleep Foundation (See Chapter 9 Notes) says to keep the room temperature at 60 to 67 degrees which they say is an ideal setting for most people. I think you can have it in the 70s in the summer if you use fans. Some people like a noisy fan to block other noises that wake them or keep them awake.

I've just discovered a free sleep app called "White Noise" on my iPhone, which I like for the different sounds to choose from. I especially like the beach and ocean sounds. If you keep the phone connected to the charger, you can have it on all night. It's also convenient to have when you have over-night travel away from home.

The comfort of mattress and pillow are important for better sleep, and most people say they sleep better when sheets and pillows have a fresh scent, so wash linens weekly, pillowcases more often. Periodically launder the mattress pad in hot water, and sprinkle the mattress with baking soda to sit for several hours before vacuuming. Sun your pillows outside when you can for a great scent that will remind some of you of when we once hung our sheets out to sun and air dry.

Pets~ if you have a pet that sleeps in the room with you, and you have insomnia, then consider having the pet sleep somewhere else. Pet lovers everywhere will have something to say about that, and I'm one of them; but if you have insomnia, you will have to consider this recommendation seriously. They need to be trained to stay quiet while you sleep.

Essential Oils--use aromatherapy oils for both the fragrance in the room and for calming purposes. Dab some oil on a tissue or cotton ball and sniff, taking 10 to 15 deep breaths. Some people use a dispenser with the oils and water spraying from it. The experts say that if you're upset about something; reach for some organic essential oils with high concentrations of lavender. It's reported to be one of nature's best sedatives. And if, when you're awake, you're stewing about work, money, or feeling overwhelmed, try other oils, e.g., frankincense and myrrh; which can slow you down to promote a heavier, more restorative sleep.

3-Foods, Drinks, and Over-the-Counter Meds: WebMD reports the effects of caffeine can last up to 24 hours, so the chances are it will affect your sleep and may also cause frequent awakenings. Alcohol may not only have a sedative effect following consumption, but it can then lead to frequent arousals and a non-restful night's sleep. Ask your doctor when decongestants and asthma inhalers, which are stimulants, can best be taken to help minimize any effect on sleep.

Some sleep experts say a late dinner or snacking before going to bed can activate the digestive system and keep you up. Especially if you have gastroesophageal reflux (GERD) or heartburn, it is even more important to avoid eating and drinking right before bed since this can make your symptoms worse. Also, drinking a lot of fluids before bed may require more frequent visits to the bathroom that can disturb your sleep.

Other sleep experts say a bedtime snack of a small bowl of low-sugar whole-grain cereal with milk is good for insomniacs. Carbs in the cereal and the tryptophan in the milk boost serotonin in the body.

More tips from the sleep experts about food, drink, and other stimulants:

NO coffee or other caffeine after noontime because of the length of time it stays in the body. Coffee has around 100 milligrams of caffeine per cup; more if you have a big mug.

NO decaf coffee after noontime. Compared to the caffeine found in a regular cup, the decaf samples have less, but some have over 20 milligrams.

Sodas—have little or preferably none after noontime. Colas and other sodas like Mountain Dew have caffeine. Some brands of root beer, one orange soda, and one cream soda have caffeine. Check the labels.

Chocolate--candy bars have some caffeine, but the darker the chocolate, the higher the caffeine content. Hershey's Special Dark Chocolate Bar has almost as much caffeine as a can of Coke.

Ice cream—a half cup of Breyer's All Natural Chocolate ice cream has only 3 milligrams of caffeine, according to a Consumer Reports analysis. Other ice creams have none. Check the labels.

Energy drinks—some of these beverages have been reformulated or pulled from shelves. Look out for this type of drink with caffeine.

An alcoholic nightcap--Tempting though it may be when you can't sleep, it can ruin your slumber—and that's especially true for women. According to one study, men who went to bed tipsy slept soundly—as well as when they were sober—but women slept fewer minutes and woke up more often. What's more, alcohol robs you of REM and the other, deeper stages of sleep—which are the ones that make you feel most rested.

Weight-loss pills--taking 1,223 milligrams in a daily dose of Zantrex-3 is like having 12 cups of coffee, according to a 2005 analysis conducted by ConsumerLab.com.

Many pain relievers incorporate caffeine to ease the pain, but if you take more than the label suggests, you could be taking more than you need. Two Excedrin Migraine tablets have 130 milligrams of caffeine, the same as a Starbucks Light Frappuccino with espresso—so it's best to stick with the two-tablets-per-24-hours label instructions.

Honey and Salt--consider this simple, two ingredient solution for getting a great night's sleep. It may help your body relax and regroup from the day and prepare itself for the next morning: Combine five teaspoons of raw organic honey and one teaspoon of pink Himalayan sea salt. Mix and store in a glass jar. You can make as much or as little as you want, but a 5:1 ratio works the best. Just put a little bit of this mixture under your tongue at night before you go to sleep and let it dissolve naturally.

This Himalayan salt and honey combination can work to increase serotonin, helping us to de-stress naturally allowing us to get the best sleep possible. This sea salt contains more than 80 minerals and elements that your body needs for different processes, aiding your body in recovering from the day. Honey contains glucose which helps in supplying our body's cells with energy.

Some alternative hot drinks to try instead of coffee or tea are: Herbal Teas - From hibiscus to mint to chamomile, the possibilities are practically endless when it comes to herbal teas. Rooibos - With its naturally sweet, woody, tobacco-y flavor, rooibos has a depth that makes it a good alternative to coffee. Roasted Grains--for an earthy, roasted flavor, try Korean and Japanese teas. White Coffee--this Lebanese after-dinner beverage is made with sweet-scented orange flower water. Ginger Honey Lemon Tonic--perfect for chilly winter days, and particularly soothing for sore throats and stomach aches.

4-Exercise--plenty of research supports the suggestion that exercise improves sleep. One study found that insomniacs who exercised regularly slept better and had more energy all day. They also reported they did not feel as depressed.

Sometimes, exercise at night can interrupt your sleep, so find a time that works for you: a morning walk or bike ride, lifting weights at home or a gym open 24/7, or a workout whenever you can find time.

Regular exercise can improve sleep quality and duration. Exercising immediately before bedtime can have a stimulating effect on the body and should be avoided. So, stop several hours before you plan to retire for the night.

Prevention Magazine has an article, "It's Time to Stop Counting Sheep" in the April 2016 issue with some new ideas to aid sleep. For example, "WHOOPS: You're wide awake at lights-out, no idea why. FIX IT: Keep those eyes open. No cheating! Keep looking at the ceiling. This little exercise is called *paradoxical intention*, and it really works, according to a study published in *Behavioral and Cognitive Psychotherapy*. Many other useful tips are in this article.

SIX SLEEP AIDS:

Relax and Sleep: This exercise will help you to let go and focus on the suggestions you give yourself. Say the following suggestions to yourself or out loud. All it requires is your concentration and imagination. If possible, commit these ideas to memory, or put them on audiotape with soft, slow background music.

I feel calm... I feel relaxed... I feel in control...
I am calm... I am relaxed... I am in control...
I feel safe... I feel secure... I'm letting go...
As I let go, all my muscle groups begin to relax...
I feel calm... I feel relaxed... I feel in control...

As my muscle groups relax, a beam of sunlight focuses on my scalp and spreads relaxation and warmth throughout my body...
It rids me of all negative thoughts and feelings...
Leaving me with only positive thoughts and feelings...
I feel calm... I feel relaxed... I feel in control...
My mind is now open to receive the helpful and beneficial suggestions I am about to give myself.
I will go to sleep quickly now. I will remain asleep during the night unless I need to wake up.

I will have a restful sleep and awaken in the morning feeling refreshed.

I feel calm… I feel relaxed… I feel in control…
I am calm… I am relaxed… I am in control.

Breathing Exercise: Close your eyes and notice your breathing. Turn all your attention to your natural breathing pattern and feel the air enter and leave your nose or mouth. Visualize the flow of air as it passes through your mouth, airways, down into your stomach, and back out again.

Survey your body for any tension, and as you exhale, feel the tension leave that part of your body. Visualize your breath reaching your forehead, your neck, your shoulders, your arms… and then releasing the tension as you exhale.

If your mind wanders to another worry or thought, let it go and gently redirect your attention back to your breath.

Guided Imagery: The idea in this exercise is to focus your attention on an image or story, so that your mind can let go of worries or thoughts that keep you awake.

Get into a comfortable position in bed. Close your eyes and relax. Begin to visualize a scene, memory, or story that you find calming. Find what works best for you by trying a few choices; for example: a favorite vacation or calming outdoor spot, a relaxing activity like curling up with a book in your favorite chair, or something repetitive like remembering the steps of an exercise or dance routine. The key is to find something that allows you to focus your attention and let go of other thoughts. Begin to create this scenario in your mind. Visualize all the details of the image or story, as slowly and carefully as you can. Any time you find your mind drifting to an irrelevant thought (a worry about the day or a "must do" for tomorrow), acknowledge it and let it go. Turn your mind's eye back to your relaxing story. It's okay if this takes time before it works, each time you practice you will get better at it.

Meditation: Count backwards from 100; if you forget your place, simply start over and keep counting down. Remember, there is no right or wrong — it's all mediating! Or concentrate on a place, color, face, etc. Allow your mind to clear and focus on a single image. Notice how this makes you feel.

Relax & Sleep Well by Glenn Harrold - The Ultimate Hypnosis & Meditation App—try this one; you'll think you've invited an Englishman into your bedroom! *www.youtube.com*

Free Sleep App on iPhone -*White Noise* – mentioned in this chapter under *sleep environment*.

POSTER
HEALTHY LIVING
Diet, Exercise, Sleep
PENN'S DOs and DON'Ts

~DO EAT MORE VEGETABLES, FRUITS, NUTS, FEWER REFINED GRAINS, AND FEWER SUGARS.

~DO PRACTICE PORTION CONTROL.

~DO HAVE A SUPPORT SYSTEM IF DIETING AND EXERCISING.

~DO KEEP A REGULAR SCHEDULE FOR EXERCISING.

~DO AVOID STRESS.

~DO GET PLENTY OF SLEEP.

~DO FOLLOW TIPS FOR INSOMNIACS.

~DO USE SLEEP AIDS as suggested in Chapter 9.

~DO LIMIT TV and ELECTRONICS AT NIGHT.

~DON'T TAKE DAY NAPS IF YOU'RE AN INSOMNIAC.

~DON'T READ AN EXCITING BOOK JUST BEFORE SLEEPTIME.

Print and post where you and others will see it.

CHECKLIST & CONTRACT

I WILL COMPLETE THIS CHECKLIST & CONTRACT
FOR EACH BEHAVIOR I WORK ON.

____ I am motivated to change/improve my behavior:
Name Behavior: **FOCUS on HEALTHY LIVING.**

____ I will begin by working to improve one behavior at a time.

____ I will complete this checklist for my behavior improvement.

____ I will sign a contract and place it where I can see it often.

____ I will work with another person to improve this behavior.

____ l will keep a journal about my progress and feelings.

____ I will read Chapters 1 & 2.

____ I will complete the worksheets for Chapters 1 & 2.

____ I will read the chapter of the behavior I want to improve.

____ I will complete the worksheet(s) relevant to this chapter.

CONTRACT

As of today, I choose to improve my life, one behavior at a time, by
Focusing ON HEALTHY LIVING.

Name_____ Date_____

Print and Post

WORKSHEET 9

HEALTHY HABITS CHECKLIST

Yes   No

___   ___   I get a physical checkup annually and see my health care provider as needed.

___   ___   I exercise 5-15 minutes or more several times a week.

___   ___   I eat a well-balanced diet at least five days a week.

___   ___   I weigh close to my ideal weight.

___   ___   I have fewer than 5 alcoholic drinks a week.

___   ___   I wear a seat belt in the car at all times.

___   ___   I do not smoke.

___   ___   I only take prescribed drugs.

___   ___   I average sleeping at least 7 hours nightly.

___   ___   I am seldom depressed.

___   ___   I seldom worry about things I can't change.

___   ___   I face up to problems and cope with change.

___   ___   I try to think positive thoughts.

___   ___   I read books and journals often.

Yes   No

___   ___   I do puzzles/games to keep my brain active.

___   ___   I choose to have an optimistic outlook on life.

___   ___   I have a friend I can talk to about my life.

___   ___   I am close with family and friends.

___   ___   I often have social or educational activities.

___   ___   I easily express healthy emotions.

___   ___   I respond to other people's feelings.

___   ___   I am comfortable with other people.

___   ___   I accept opinions of others.

___   ___   I stick up for myself when necessary.

___   ___   I pray or meditate regularly.

___   ___   I participate in spiritual rituals with others.

___   ___   I know and accept my limitations.

___   ___   I can make decisions for my life.

___   ___   I offer my time and assets to help others.

___   ___   I quickly forgive myself and others.

Count your YES responses.

Healthy Habits Score _____

How to interpret your score:

Your YES responses on the Healthy Habit Checklist provide an idea of how well you take care of your health.

25 and above--Excellent: You're doing a great job of taking care of your health.

16-24--Average: You can do better to have good health.

15 and below--Poor: Bad habits may diminish your health.

Sharon W. Penn 2017 Change 1 Behavior, Improve Your Life.
Email me: sharonwpenn@gmail.com

Chapter 10

Behavior Change:
Treasure Your Friendships

"One of the most beautiful qualities of true friendship is to
understand and to be understood."
L.A.Seneca

Real friends are needed to enjoy life to the fullest. As William Penn
said, "A true friend unbusoms (discloses) freely, advises justly, assists
readily, adventures boldly, takes all patiently, defends courageously, and
continues a friend unchangeably."

The human being is a social creature; it's in our nature to be in
relationships with others. Positive relationships are crucial for physical
and mental well-being; in fact, loneliness is toxic. And it's the quality
of our connections with others that profoundly affects us.

There are two requirements for stable friendships: regular contact
and a persistent demonstration of caring. We need to belong and to be
reassured that we belong. No matter how busy our lives, we need to
keep social contacts and friendships a top priority. Again, friendships
are a necessity.

In our busy world today, it's hard to keep friends. Before you
know it, weeks or months have passed, and you have not been in contact
with your dearest friends. They are as busy as you are. So, unless you
have friends who are super diligent about keeping in touch, you'll have

to be the one to call, text, or email. Oh, sure, you're probably friends on Facebook, but your best friends deserve a personal message from you often. Here are some ideas for maintaining that special bonding with someone:

If you want to keep a good friend or revive a friendship, you've got to set aside the time. Psychology Today says, "Since intimacy is the keystone of friendship, tell your friends how you feel, that you miss him/her, and don't want to let this friendship slip away."

Email is the obvious easy way to keep in touch, but the phone may be better for some people. Some, nowadays, prefer to text rather than call. If you have to put it on your calendar to remind yourself to call, email, or text your close friends a few times a month, do it. And, put his/her number on speed dial. Since some people like emails or texts more than phone calls, find out which they like best.

If you live close to each other, arrange a standing coffee or lunch date. If the friend lives out of town, make an effort to visit each other once a year or so.

Our friends are often those with whom we cross paths regularly. Our friends tend to be neighbors, coworkers, classmates, church members, and people we meet up with in classes we take. As you make new friends, this may be the place to direct you to Chapter 4-*Convey Your Approachability to Others,* which fits in with this chapter.

How do we choose our friends? How do we choose one person in our writing class, yoga class, workplace, or neighbor, and not another? We may be responding to their overtures of friendship as you find in Chapter 4. We may have things in common once we know something about them.

To transition from acquaintanceship to friendship is characterized by an increase in self-disclosure. One person risks telling personal information and then waits for the other to do the same. Reciprocity is the key to continuing the transition. Think about some of the friendships you have; don't you and the friend have an understanding of what to say when responding to the other person's personal information?

Some key ingredients in developing these satisfying friendships are emotional expressiveness and unconditional support followed by acceptance, loyalty, and trust. Our real friends are there for us but rarely cross the line--a friend with too many negative opinions about our clothes, our choice of partners, or our taste in movies and art will not be a friend for long.

And, it's the giving and not receiving that makes us value a friend more. Ben Franklin said: "He that has once done you a kindness will be more ready to do you another than he whom you yourself have obliged." This quote is known as the Ben Franklin Effect. So, let your friends do things for you as well as being generous yourself toward them.

Some researchers who study friendship say certain behaviors are necessary to maintain the attachment bond: We have to be willing to tell them what's happening in our life and to listen to them about their life. Then we have to be prepared to support them if they need us.

We need to write, call, visit--meet the easiest way to take the time to catch up. The important thing is to interact. Having a frequent email correspondence or telephone call or text may often be as good as being there.

The important part of friendship is that we must enjoy and feel good about it. The real test of the friendship is that we will be willing to expend the energy it takes to keep it alive.

TIPS--Let's put all the tips together, check off the ones you already do, then star* the ones you want to do first, and with what friend:

- Regular contact—schedule friends on your calendar.
- Return calls and texts within 24 hours, sooner, if possible
- Show friends that you care about them.
- Be a good listener—ask questions, and don't try to top their stories with yours.
- Share feelings.
- Exchange histories.
- Confide private thoughts, needs, and fears.
- Whatever you want, ask for it directly.
- Plan activities together.

- Honesty isn't always best—if it's too painful or will destroy the friendship, don't do it.
- Friendship is equality--If you're doing most of the giving, back off.
- Be proactive—go out and find new friends to add to your other friends.
- Carefully assess before you commit to a new person—are you eager to see this person? Do you respect him/her? Are you interested in his/her mind, experiences, and problems?
- And, never, ever, betray a confidence.

POSTER
FRIENDSHIPS
PENN'S DOs and DON'Ts

-DO PLAN ACTIVITIES WITH FRIENDS.

-DO GIVE UNCONDITIONAL SUPPORT.

-DO GIVE ACCEPTANCE, LOYALTY, and TRUST.

-DO SHARE YOUR LIFE WITH FRIENDS.

-DO LISTEN TO THEM.

-DO INTERACT- WRITE, CALL, or VISIT.

-DO CONFIDE THOUGHTS, NEEDS, FEELINGS, and FEARS.

-DO ASK FOR WHAT YOU WANT.

-DO ADD NEW FRIENDS TO YOUR CIRCLE; ASSESS THEM CAREFULLY.

-DON'T CRITICIZE THEM.

-DON'T DO ALL THE GIVING.

-DON'T EVER BETRAY A CONFIDENCE.

Print and post where you and others will see it.

CHECKLIST & CONTRACT

I WILL COMPLETE THIS CHECKLIST & CONTRACT
FOR EACH BEHAVIOR I WORK ON.

____ I am motivated to change/improve my behavior:
Name Behavior: **TREASURE MY FRIENDSHIPS**.

____ I will begin by working to improve one behavior at a time.

____ I will complete this checklist for my behavior improvement.

____ I will sign a contract and place it where I can see it often.

____ I will work with another person to improve this behavior.

____ I will keep a journal about my progress and feelings.

____ I will read Chapters 1 & 2.

____ I will complete the worksheets for Chapters 1 & 2.

____ I will read the chapter of the behavior I want to improve.

____ I will complete the worksheet(s) relevant to this behavior.

CONTRACT

As of today, I choose to improve my life, one behavior at a time, by **Treasuring My FRIENDSHIPS**.

Name_____ Date_____

Print and Post

WORKSHEET 10

FRIENDSHIPS CHECKLIST

Use these tasks to make and keep friends. This checklist is also used in Chapter 4 to become more approachable.

7 Daily Tasks   Times Tried (2-10 daily)

1-Smile Appropriately---

2-Make Eye Contact---

3-Greet/Get Response---

4-Touch Appropriately---

5-Use Open Body Language---

6-Compliment Others---

7-Say name in conversation---

Please tell me about your experiences.
Email me: *sharonwpenn@gmail.com*

Chapter 11

Behavior Change:
Choose To Age Gracefully:
Attitude, Memory, Pain

"There is a fountain of youth: it is your mind, your talents,
the creativity you bring t your life and the lives of people
you love. When you learn to tap this source, you will truly
have defeated age." Sophia Loren

Improve Your Attitude

My very favorite saying since taking a philosophy course in college is about attitude, by Viktor Frankl, who was a psychiatrist in Vienna.

In 1942, during World War II, Dr. Frankl, his wife, and his parents were deported to a Nazi ghetto. There Dr. Frankl suffered unspeakable atrocities, and then later was liberated by the Americans in 1945. Only he and a sister, who had earlier escaped to Austria, survived. While suffering abuse in the concentration camps, he came to believe that **"Everything can be taken from a man but one thing: the last of the human freedoms—to choose one's attitude in any given set of circumstances, to choose one's own way."**

Charles Swindoll, a pastor and writer, says, "The remarkable thing is, we have a choice every day regarding the attitude we will embrace for that day."

And…"We cannot change the fact that people will act in a certain way. We cannot change the inevitable. The only thing we can do is play on the one string we have…That is our attitude. I am convinced that life is 10% what happens to me and 90% how I react to it. And so it is with you…We are in charge of our attitude."

"You're only as old as you feel" may be truer than we used to think. It's getting a second look from the science field today as more people are aging than ever before because of the baby boomers. There's some interesting research about attitudes from Yale University and the National Institute on Aging. Use a search engine to check out their websites.

Melinda Beck writes in the Wall Street Journal (Oct 17, 2009) that a social psychologist, Becca R. Levy, Ph.D., and colleagues looked at surveys taken by 386 men and women in 1968, when they were under age 50, and then studied their subsequent health records. Nearly four decades later, the subjects who had held the most negative stereotypes about older people (answering "true" to statements such as "older people are…feeble… helpless…absent-minded…make too many mistakes") were significantly more likely to have had heart attacks or strokes than those who held more positive views. In the negative group, 25% had cardiovascular events, versus 13% of the positive group.

In another study of Dr. Levy's, of 660 people over 50 years old, those who in 1975 viewed aging as a positive experience lived an average of 7.5 years longer than those with more negative views. These researchers found that the people who had more positive perceptions of aging in 1975 were significantly likely to practice better health behaviors during the next 20 years—including visiting the doctor more regularly, eating a balanced diet, maintaining a desired weight, using a seatbelt and avoiding tobacco.

"Our study carries two messages," say Dr. Levy and her colleagues. "The discouraging one is that negative self-perceptions can diminish life expectancy; the encouraging one is that positive self-perceptions can prolong life expectancy."

Channe Fodeman, a clinical social worker, recently moderated a panel: "So This is What 90 Looks Like." Five nonagenarians were asked to explain their longevity and good health, and each one mentioned attitude—not dwelling on being older or what they couldn't do, or on themselves too much.

"A healthy attitude is contagious but don't wait to catch it
from others. Be a carrier."
Tom Stoppard

Improve Your Memory

Memory has always been a serious subject, even though we joke about it when we fail to remember a name, place, or an item on our to-do list. It becomes a more serious subject as we age, and as large numbers of baby boomers are taking longer to remember and retrieve things that used to be readily available to them in their memories.

In this book, Chapter 2-*Why It's Hard to Change a Habit, and How to Do It Anyway!* will give you a good picture of how the brain works to use your memory. So, as a supplement to that, in this chapter, I will be giving you TIPS to help you preserve the memory you have and TIPS to help remember and retrieve quickly what you're searching for. Please share any tips you have at my Email: *sharonwpenn@gmail.com*

Tips to Preserve Your Memory:

Eat well to maximize brain health: lean proteins, (chicken and fish), healthy fats (olive and canola oils), good carbs (fruits, veggies, whole grains).

Have a little red wine or champagne. Research is showing that both of these drinks have benefits with memory, and possibly, with Alzheimer's disease. One drink a day may be helpful with memory, but more than that is toxic to neurons and a risk for memory loss.

Pay close attention to your body numbers and keep them at normal levels. Blood pressure, blood sugar, blood cholesterol levels, and weight.

Get calm. Meditation, yoga, relaxation methods, prayer, and just sitting or lying in a quiet room is refreshing. Schedule it.

Stay calm. Trying to do too much for too many people is stressful, so pace yourself. Say "NO" to some things--drop some things or share some chores with others.

Think positive. Every day, think of people and things you're grateful for. It helps to remember by writing them down.

Get plenty of sleep. Harvard Medical researchers found that finding creative solutions to problems depends on sleep: the sleeping brain is vastly capable of synthesizing complex information. If you have trouble going to sleep or staying asleep, please see Chapter 9-Focus on Healthy Living: Diet, Exercise, Sleep.

Don't smoke, and, if you do, please stop now. Have you ever heard of anybody who benefits from smoking? The illnesses that smokers get probably contribute to poorer brain function. There are proven ways and aids to help you stop smoking; all you need is the motivation. Please, please, do it now.

Be more social and have more fun. There are numerous reasons to have contacts with other people—more stimulating intellectual activities and discussions with others promote healthy memory function; support during stressful times; and ideas from others to have more fun.

Exercise your body. Many medical doctors recommend both aerobics and weight training, so have a safe plan in place when you start and start slowly. Most people know they need to exercise, but not everyone knows what it does for their brain. Exercise increases capillary development in the brain, meaning more blood supply, more nutrients, and more oxygen.

On his website, Dr. Joseph Mercola reports, "Exercise helps protect and improve your brain function; he gives ways this occurs. *www. mercola.com*

Prevention Magazine has some strength-training and aerobic exercises that you can do from your chair which is both good for older people who have balance problems; and younger adults who are just starting an exercise program. These are found in the monthly magazine for August 2015.

One year-long study found that adults who regularly exercised were enlarging their brain's memory center by one to two percent per year, where typically that center shrinks with age. Other studies show that exercise helps slow down and even reverse some diseases, including type 2 diabetes, osteoporosis, and heart disease. And, contrary to popular belief, strength training is particularly important for the elderly.

By strengthening muscles, connective tissues, tendons, and ligaments, strength training helps you maintain a stable body position, and allows you to perform everyday activities like climbing stairs and getting out of a chair with greater ease. This freedom of movement adds to your quality of life, but the benefits don't end there. One study showed that strength training in the elderly genetically turned back the biological clock about ten years—an excellent bit of information.

Other Ways to Exercise Your Mind. You can train your brain to be faster and sharper by:

- **Switching hands to eat** with your non-prominent hand at one meal a day
- **Working crossword puzzles, games, and computer brain games**
- **Playing ping-pong or riding bicycles** with someone who encourages you to increase your pace.

I attended an excellent seminar in 2011, *"Protecting the Aging Brain: Focus on Nutrition and Mind/Body Health,"* presented by Gary W. Arendash, Ph.D. Please see Chapter 11 Notes.

He shared eight strategies for optimizing brain function over the life span:

- **High intake of brain nutrients** from both food and supplements throughout life
- **Physical activity** (exercise) throughout life
- **Intellectual and Cognitive activities** throughout life
- **Modest caloric intake and low saturated fat intake**
- **Maintain normal blood pressure** (especially systolic)

- **Keep cholesterol levels within normal range**
- **Avoid chronic stress**
- **Caffeine intake daily!** (at the time of the seminar, Dr. A. said he drank about five cups of coffee a day; that's his exclamation point).

Dr. Arendash also gave us memory enhancement strategies:

> **Eliminate non-essential material:**
> Memory space is scarce and thus precious.
> Don't remember certain things. Items that can be recalled via notes, references, etc. should not be remembered.

> **Facilitate attention:**
> -Reduce unwanted visual, auditory, and anxiety-relevant distractions.
> -Organize and control your learning/memory environment.
> -If necessary, use earplugs to reduce noise.
> -Use relaxation techniques to reduce anxiety and stress (stretching exercise is useful to reduce muscle tension).

> **Maintain task focus** by being "simple-minded." If going into another room to get something, complete that task before being distracted by another task.

> **Maximize depth of cognitive processing:**
> Think about the significance of new material being processed. Elaborate and make connections (how does the new information fit in with what you already know?).

> **Optimize the timing of learning/memory:**
> Study consistently to assure that short-term memory (over minutes) and long-term memory (over days or more) of the material are consistent. (Review material multiple times for memory encoding.)

Space study periods, providing at least 10 minutes per hour for rest. Distribute material to be memorized over several shorter study periods (avoid cramming).

> **Rehearse to facilitate transfer from short-term to long-term memory:**
Use successively longer intervals (i.e., repeat after 10 seconds, then 30 seconds, then 2 minutes, etc.).

> **Use external memory aids:**
Take notes, keep records in one place so you don't forget where you put them.
Put objects or notes in prominent place where they cannot be overlooked. -Link new tasks to old habit: e.g., place pill to be taken in the morning next to toothbrush.

> **Develop "habits of remembering" (procedural memory):**
If you frequently lock yourself out of your house because of forgetting your keys: Develop habit of having keys in your hand before closing the door to the house.
- This may initially require active attention and perhaps external cues (e.g., large sign on the door saying "keys in hand").
- With sufficient practice, procedure should become an "automatic" habit.

> **Explore your learning/memory style:**
Discover how you learn best (listening, reading, writing, etc.). Practice using different approaches to optimize your learning mode.
Study with friends who have complementary styles of learning (you may benefit from each other).

> **Use associative techniques to facilitate encoding and retrieval:**
Verbal-image associations- (Remember the capital of Maryland is Annapolis by thinking of Mary landing on an apple).

Verbal-verbal associations- (Mnemonics such as jingles to help memorize a list of terms in order (e.g., "On Old Olympus Towering Top..." for olfactory, optic, oculomotor, trachea, etc.).

> **For remembering names:**
> Look directly at the person, say the name aloud as soon as you are introduced.
> Rehearse the name at successively longer intervals.
> Look for the most memorable feature and associate that with the name.
> Invent a feature with the name (Zuckerman=sucker man-imagine the man with an all-day sucker).

> **Organize material by:**
> Categorizing information.
> Outlining information.
> Explaining or teaching the information to someone else.

> **If you can't remember everything, focus on the important information.** See Chapter 11 Notes
> Arendash 2011

More Tips to Remember and Retrieve Items in Your Memory:

Recommended Reading: In my library, I have a great book about memory by Joshua Foer, *Moonwalking with Einstein: The Art and Science of Remembering Everything* (2011). In addition to learning memory aids (which he tells us about) so he could (and did) win the U.S. Memory Championship, Foer traveled around the country meeting interesting people. Among others, there was an elderly, personable man with a severe case of amnesia, a savant who claims to have memorized 9,000 books, and a high school history teacher who uses 2500-year-old memory techniques to help his students on the state Regent exam.

Foer learned that by using our spatial memory we can memorize long lists of items. He gives us tips that will help some of us remember things for many years to come, if not forever.

More Memory Tips

Make a memory notebook, either in a spiral notebook, smartphone, or on your computer, or some to go in one; some to go in the other. Start by putting in: phone numbers, email addresses, physical addresses, medical info, inspirational thoughts, quotes, to-do lists, birthdays, a grocery list, and gratitude lists of people and things for which you are grateful. You will think of others as you make these lists. Writing it down helps you to remember, and then look at your list several times a day to confirm it.

Post reminder signs all around your house, car, or office. Use Post-it notes in several colors. Cute ones are fun for all. Choose one color to show "urgent" or "priority."

Bundle items from your to-do list: Always call or email someone--your mom or favorite aunt or a shut-in when you wash your hands. Or replace the batteries in your smoke detectors when you change the clocks to or from daylight-saving time.

Exercise your mind: reading, playing a musical instrument, playing cards or games, watching quiz shows, working crossword puzzles or word games.

Learn and use mnemonic tricks: rhymes, acronyms, words that spell lists, and others. One I use when I'm turning something on or off—"righty-tighty, lefty-loosey." When learning the piano keys—sharps: Every Good Boy Does Fine; flats: FACE. And make up some of your own.

And finally; one I especially like for everyone to have for your safety: ***Remember to put your car keys beside your bed at night. If you are alone and hear a noise outside your home or someone trying to get in your house, just press the panic button for your car. The alarm will be set off, and the horn will continue to sound until either you turn it off, or the car battery dies.***

Next time you come home and you start to put your keys away, think of this: It's a security alarm system that you probably already have and requires no installation. Test it. It will go off from most everywhere inside your house and will keep honking until your battery runs down or until you reset it with the button on the key fob chain (know where the reset button is before you test it). It works if you park in your driveway or garage.

If your car alarm goes off when someone is trying to break into your house, odds are the intruder won't stick around. After a few seconds, all the neighbors will be looking out their windows to see who is out there, and sure enough, the criminal won't want that. And remember to carry your keys while walking to your car in a parking lot; the alarm can work the same way there. Share this protective tip with everyone. Maybe it could save a life or prevent a sexual abuse crime.

It would also be useful for any emergency, such as a heart attack, when you can't reach a phone. Carry you car keys when you go outside; in case of a fall, the neighbors will hear when you activate the car alarm and know there's a problem. Having your keys with you may save a life!

Improve Your Pain Management

Older Americans complain the most about pain, and many take painkillers regularly, with acetaminophen taken the most for mild or moderate pain. Research shows liver damage from acetaminophen for some people. They get damage to the stomach lining which can lead to blood loss from the troubled area, stomach pains (gastritis), and even ulcers. Other research shows using both aspirin and ibuprofen or naproxen at the same time can cause risk. Discuss painkiller side effects with your doctor, and search online at websites like WebMD and Mayo for more help, if needed after reading this. I don't think we can know too much about our health and the health of our loved ones.

Alternative Treatments for Chronic Pain

Some better pain-relievers that don't have the side effects of over-the-counter drugs are:

Acupuncture is becoming an accepted treatment for pain. Studies have found that it works for pain caused by many conditions, including fibromyalgia, osteoarthritis, back injuries, and sports injuries.

Many doctors say there's enough scientific evidence for acupuncture and they prescribe it. In my area of Central Florida, one healing center offers free ear acupuncture sessions to help reduce stress. Check your area.

Biofeedback. You can learn how to control unconscious bodily functions, like blood pressure or your heart rate, with this method. It can help with headache pain, fibromyalgia, and other conditions.

Chiropractic manipulation has become a more accepted treatment over the past years, especially for lower back pain.

Exercise. Regular physical activity benefits people who have many different painful conditions. Always check with a doctor before starting any form of exercise, especially if you are in pain. Your doctor will have an opinion as to whether this a good time for you to start this activity; and it you can, what form to take and how to get started.

Guided imagery can help with pain from headaches, cancer, osteoarthritis, and fibromyalgia. An expert teaches ways to direct thoughts by focusing on specific images.

Hypnosis. Studies have found this approach helpful with different sorts of pain like back pain, repetitive strain injuries, and cancer pain. It's best to use a certified hypnotist or a psychotherapist who has experience in hypnosis. You probably don't want to use someone whose only experience is at parties having someone "quack like a duck" while the subject is under hypnosis.

Marijuana. There's substantial evidence that marijuana has a modest effect on certain types of nerve pain. Marijuana can help chemotherapy patients. Now, that medical marijuana is available in some states, sick people in those states don't have to obtain it illegally. Marijuana does have risks, and I hear the risks can be severe, including addiction and psychosis; so talk to your doctor if you're considering the use of marijuana to find out about the risks and the laws regarding the use of medical marijuana in your state. Pharmaceutical cannabinoids derived from the active ingredient of marijuana are sometimes used for pain.

Massage. It's so relaxing, and it can ease pain from rheumatoid arthritis, neck and back injuries, and fibromyalgia. Once you try it with a certified massage therapist, you'll never hesitate to go to one when you're in pain again.

Meditation. Supposedly, meditators process pain differently than non-meditators. Meditators pay more attention to the direct sensation of pain, where non-meditators show more activity in areas associated with evaluation and language. It's the inner dialogue of "That hurts! I'm such a klutz! This stinks! When is it going to stop?" Interestingly, the more a meditator's brain focuses on the pain experience and the less activity in the evaluation system, the higher their pain tolerance for some people.

Music therapy. Studies have found it can help with osteoarthritis, cancer pain, and other pains that work by helping the patient to relax.

Psychotherapy. Cognitive behavioral therapy is one method that therapists use when treating chronic pain. It helps people identify and change the thought and behavior patterns that contribute to their unhappiness. As mentioned earlier, hypnosis can temporarily stop the pain. Note: Only consult a psychotherapist about pain when your doctor has ruled out any physical reasons for the pain and is in agreement with the psychotherapy.

Relaxation Therapy helps people calm themselves and release tension, which might also reduce pain. Some approaches teach people how to focus on their breathing. Many people have used relaxation therapy for fibromyalgia, headache, osteoarthritis, and other conditions.

There is a difference between Relaxation Therapy and Meditation. Meditation often produces deep relaxation and is much more effective at reducing mental and physical stress than general relaxation techniques. People who practice meditation report reduced anxiety, greater personal clarity, higher overall satisfaction with their life and greater happiness. The same response is not reported from people who practice relaxation only.

Stress-reduction techniques. Reducing stress is crucial in pain management. Some approaches used: exercise, guided imagery, hypnosis, massage, music therapy, relaxation therapy, and yoga.

Yoga can help with pain, e.g., fibromyalgia, neck pain, back pain, and arthritis. Some doctors have recommended yoga for pain for many years.

Sharon W. Penn

POSTER
AGING GRACEFULLY
PENN'S DOs and DON'Ts

~DO CHOOSE YOUR ATTITUDE.

~DO FOCUS ON YOUR HEALTH.

~DO PRESERVE YOUR MEMORY.

~DO MANAGE YOUR PAIN.

~DO RELAXATION TECHNIQUES.

~DO KEEP SAFETY IN MIND.

~DO HAVE FUN and BE SOCIAL.

~DO SEEK YOUR SPIRITUALITY.

~DON'T OVEREAT.

~DON'T SMOKE.

~DON'T ALLOW STRESS.

~DON'T ABUSE ALCOHOL OR DRUGS.

Print and post where you and others will see it.

CHECKLIST & CONTRACT

I WILL COMPLETE THIS CHECKLIST & CONTRACT FOR EACH BEHAVIOR I WORK

____ I am motivated to change/improve my behavior.
Name behavior: **CHOOSE TO AGE GRACEFULLY**

____ I will begin by working to improve one behavior at a time.

____ I will complete this checklist for each behavior.

____ I will sign a contract and place it where I can see it often.

____ I will work with another person to improve this behavior.

____ I will keep a journal about my progress and feelings.

____ I will read Chapters 1 & 2.

____ I will complete the worksheets for Chapters 1 & 2.

____ I will read the chapter of the behavior I want to improve.

____ I will complete the worksheet(s) relevant to the behavior.

CONTRACT

As of today, I choose to improve my life, one behavior at a time, by **Choosing TO AGE GRACEFULLY.**

Name_____ Date_____

Print and Post

WORKSHEET 11

AGE GRACEFULLY RATING

Use the scale below to answer the 16 questions, based on the past month.

N=Never　　　　**R=Rarely**　　　　**S=Sometimes**
　　　O=Often　　　　**M=Most of the time**

1~ Do you present a positive attitude of yourself to others? _____

2~ Do you write your thoughts in a journal? If so, do you make a list of things and people that you are grateful for, and keep it current? _____

3~ Do you begin and/or end your day with a minute of deep breathing, and focus awareness of your body, thoughts, and feelings? _____

4~ Do you pray or meditate, and experience the activity with attentiveness? _____

5~ Do you spend quality time by hanging out with people you love or admire? _____

6~ If someone you love or admire lives far away, do you call, text, or e-mail them? _____

7~ Do you do something to energize your body, e.g., stretching, walking, swimming, shaking your body to your favorite dance music, or some other fun physical activity? _____

8~ Do you focus on your health by proper eating, getting enough sleep, and drinking lots of filtered water? _____

9~ Do you try new things, e.g., a new hobby, a new skill, or make an effort to meet new people, or other new thing? _____

10~ Do you regularly declutter your living or workspace? _____

11~ Do you keep your brain active by doing puzzles, crosswords, reading, etc? _____

12~ Do you avoid excessive sun exposure and use sunscreen daily? _____

13~ Do you dress to suit your age? _____

14~ Do you avoid too much stress in your life? _____

15~ When you do have ongoing stress, do you practice calming yourself with prayer, meditation, yoga, exercise, walk outside, talk with someone, etc? _____

16~ If you don't have someone to take care of, do you have a pet or pets? _____

Total: **Never** ____   **Rarely** ____   **Sometimes**____
                 Often ____   **Most of the time** ____

If you put *Often* or *Most of the time* on 7 or more questions, you may be aging gracefully.

If fewer than that, look at the questions you reported *Never, Rarely, or Sometimes;* and decide right now to do one of these at a time and make it a habit by doing it *Often* or *Most of the Time.*

Sharon W. Penn 2017 Change 1 Behavior, Improve Your Life.

Email me: sharonwpenn@gmail.com

Chapter 12

Behavior Change:
Seek Your Spirituality

"Just as a candle cannot burn without fire,
man cannot live without a spiritual life."
Buddha

What does spirituality mean to you? Is it religious? When people say they are spiritual but not religious, what do they mean?

Deepak Chopra, a writer and a promoter of modern forms of spirituality, says, "Enlightened leadership is spiritual if we understand spirituality not as some religious dogma or ideology but as the domain of awareness where we experience values like truth, goodness, beauty, love and compassion, and also intuition, creativity, insight and focused attention."

In researching spirituality, I have found that it has many perspectives. Some of us seek the meaning of it because it gives us a sense of connection to something larger than ourselves. We seem to be searching for meaning in life, and so it is something that touches us all.

I have a spirituality test at the end of this chapter, and also in the Worksheet Section. Please let me know how you rate yourself and if you agree with your results. *Email me: sharonwpenn@gmail.com*

Research shows that meditation, prayer, and other spiritual practices seem to reveal a life force, the existence of energy fields around living organisms. I'll cover two of the spiritual practices here—meditation and prayer.

Meditation is the conscious decision to quiet the mind by focusing on one thing. We can train our conscious mind to be still and tranquil. With this come many benefits on all levels: emotional, mental, physical and spiritual. We meditate for many different reasons: to reduce stress and anxiety; to feel more relaxed and peaceful; to increase our self-awareness; to improve our general health; for spiritual connection and growth; and as a way to release stored emotions.

There are apps on your smartphone to help you meditate. Using one of these may be an easy way to start meditating. Some of the apps are free, and some are free to try.

When we meditate, our breathing slows down and becomes very shallow; and we focus inward rather than outward. We experience being in the present moment. We turn away from all of the outer distractions in life. Instead, we let go of all our outer thoughts and begin to experience the stillness of our inner life force.

When people first start meditating, some will instantly feel relaxed, quieting their mind. Others find it difficult, with the thoughts continuing to distract them. When it comes to meditating, if your thoughts don't slow down in the beginning, you're still meditating, and you are still gaining benefits.

The process of meditation is about observing these interfering thoughts, acknowledging them without emotion and then allowing them to drift away. Soon you will begin to experience quiet spaces in between the thoughts. And these will gradually get a bit longer and longer.

TO BEGIN MEDITATING, get ready by finding a quiet and comfortable spot where you will have no distractions. Choose a comfortable chair with your back straight and your feet flat on the floor, or recline or sit cross-legged on the floor. Have loose clothing on and take off your shoes, if you want to.

First, relax, and close your eyes. Take slow, deep breaths. Let the muscles in your body relax, first, the ones around your face, neck, and shoulders. Then, allow the rest of your muscles to relax, focusing on the muscles in the arms, chest, stomach, legs, and feet. Breathe slowly and naturally.

Focused meditation is one type where you choose to focus on only one thing, which will help you to quiet your mind. You will not be able to stay entirely focused during the entire meditation. You will probably only be focused for a few moments when you will lose it as a thought comes into your mind. You can then bring yourself back to your focus of interest again, as many times as you need to.

Find a center of attention by trying several of the following types at different meditation times:

FOCUS YOUR ATTENTION ON BREATH AS YOU BREATHE slowly and naturally. Feel the fresh air in your nose as you inhale, then feel your lungs and abdomen expand. When you exhale, feel the warm air in your nose as your chest deflates. Allow yourself to become totally involved in the process of breathing.

FOCUS ON A WORD OR MANTRA: choose a word like 'LOVE' 'CALM' 'BEAUTY' 'RELAX' or 'OM'-a mantra that represents the many aspects of God. Focus your attention on your slowed-down breathing pattern and with each out breath repeat your word or mantra. You may choose to say it to yourself, or you may say it out loud.

FOCUS ON THE IMAGE OF AN OBJECT: concentrate on any object that feels right to you--a beach or mountain scene, or a flower or candle. Let it come to your mind and focus on the place or object; notice all details and surrounding scenery, how it feels or how it smells.

CONCENTRATE ON THE REAL OBJECT: If you meditate outdoors, you can focus on one thing like a slight breeze or the sun on your face.

Just remember, as you focus it's normal for many other thoughts, images or feelings to come into your mind; so bring yourself back to your object of concentration. Just acknowledge the presence of these ideas and let them drift away. Do not hang on to them.

Meditate for about 20 minutes. Afterwards, sit quietly with your eyes closed for two more minutes to return to normal alertness. If you have any unusual insights, write them in a journal.

Even if you don't have insights or a unique experience, or you have interrupting thoughts, your meditation has been successful. If you let the thoughts drift away means you have benefited from this meditation.

PRAYER and HEALING: Scientific studies have shown that prayer is an important factor in living longer and staying healthy. Prayer is the most extensive alternative therapy in America today. Over 85 percent of people confronting a major illness pray, according to a University of Rochester study; and the evidence is that prayer works.

According to research findings, a broad range of spiritual practices helps alleviate stress, which is a major risk factor for disease. Religious practices are powerful ways to maintain a positive outlook when we face life's trials which come to all of us.

Dr. Herbert Benson, a cardiologist at Harvard Medical School, wrote a book called The Relaxation Response (1975). He said the relaxation response occurs when we pray. All the body's systems slow down, and our breath becomes calmer; which correlates with slower brain waves, and peace of mind. This is important to know because many doctor appointments in the U.S. today are due to headaches, backaches, stomachaches, ulcers, and depression, etc., that may be caused by stress and anxiety.

At the University of Pennsylvania, one study found that prayer and meditation increase levels of dopamine, which is associated with states of well-being.

Studies at Bowling Green State University had people who suffer migraine headaches meditate 20 minutes each day repeating "God is good. God is peace. God is love." Another group said "Grass is green. Sand is soft." The spiritual mediators had fewer headaches and more tolerance of pain than those who had focused on the neutral phrases.

Other studies: In one National Institutes of Health study, people who prayed daily had 40 percent less high blood pressure than those who did not pray daily. At Dartmouth Medical School, research found patients who had strong religious beliefs were three times more likely to recover from elective heart surgery than those who were less religious.

Young people with asthma who prayed and meditated were found by researchers at the University of Cincinnati to experience fewer symptoms than those who had not.

The Journal of Gerontology reported people who prayed or meditated coped better with illness and lived longer than those who did not.

How does prayer impact our health? The most recent research suggests that long-term daily spiritual practices help to deactivate genes that trigger inflammation.

What is the proper way to pray? Philippians 4:6-7 (King James Bible) tells us to pray without being anxious, pray about everything, and pray with grateful hearts. The proper way to pray is to pour out our hearts to God, being honest and open with God, as He already knows us better than we know ourselves. We are to present our requests to God, keeping in mind God knows what is best and will not grant a request that is not His will for us. We are to express our love, gratitude, and worship to God in prayer without worrying about having just the right words to say. God is more interested in the content of our hearts than the eloquence of our words.

We can pray by sitting, standing, or kneeling; hands open or closed; eyes opened or closed; in a church, at home, or outside; in the morning or at night—these are all side issues, subject to personal preference, conviction, and appropriateness. God's desire is for prayer to be a real and personal connection between Him and us.

The Bible gives a guide for prayer in the Lord's Prayer--Matthew 6:9-13 (King James Bible). On the website, www.gotquestions.org, the writer says The Lord's Prayer is an example of the things that should go into a prayer—worship, trust in God, requests, confession, and submission. We are to pray for the things the Lord's Prayer talks about, using our words and customizing it to our journey with God.

Prayer is not merely a technique to heal illness and promote physical health; it aims to connect the individual with God or a Higher Power, to open us to the Divinity dwelling within the self, and to make one fully present to life in the here and now.

Spiritual practitioners in different religious traditions report a sense of deep peace and radiant well-being which are not testable by scientific means (at this time). What science can tell us is that people who pray tend to be statistically healthier and live longer than those who do not.

"The essential lesson I've learned in life is to just be yourself.
Treasure the magnificent being that you are and recognize
first and foremost you're not here as a human being only.
You're a spiritual being having a human experience."
Wayne Dyer, Ph.D.

"The fact that I can plant a seed and it becomes a flower,
share a bit of knowledge and it becomes another's,
smile at someone and receive a smile in return,
are to me continual spiritual exercises."
Leo Buscaglia, Ph.D.

POSTER
SPIRITUALITY
PENN'S DOs and DON'Ts

-DO know you are a spiritual being having a human experience.

-DO keep your life's purpose in mind when decision making.

-DO connect to the spiritual aspects of life.

-DO offer your time and possessions to help protect people, animals, and plants.

-DO stay close and connected to people around you.

-DO participate in a church, or a spiritual or religious community or group.

-DO pray, do yoga, or meditate daily.

-DO trust your feelings more than logical reasons.

-DON'T FORGET- do only one behavior at a time when making a change.

Print and post where you and others will see it.

CHECKLIST & CONTRACT

I WILL COMPLETE THIS CHECKLIST & CONTRACT
FOR EACH BEHAVIOR I WORK ON.

____ I am motivated to change/improve my behavior:
Name Behavior: **Seeking My Spirituality.**

____ I will begin by working to improve one behavior at a time.

____ I will complete this checklist for my behavior improvement.

____ I will sign a contract and place it where I can see it often.

____ I will work with another person to improve this behavior.

____ I will keep a journal about my progress and feelings.

____ I will read Chapters 1 & 2.

____ I will complete the worksheets for Chapters 1 & 2.

____ I will read the chapter of the behavior I want to improve.

____ I will complete the worksheet(s) relevant to this behavior.

CONTRACT

As of today, I choose to improve my life, one behavior at a time, by
Seeking My Spirituality.

Name_____ Date_____

Print and Post

WORKSHEET 12

ARE YOU SPIRITUAL?

For a spirituality rating, please use this scale to respond:

Never=1   **Rarely=2**   **Sometimes=3**
Often=4   **Most of the time=5**

I feel connected to the spiritual aspects of life. ____

I am interested in things in life that cannot be scientifically explained. ____

I offer my time and possessions to help others. ____

I help protect people, animals, and plants. ____

I feel connected to nature. ____

I pray, do yoga, or meditate. ____

I participate in a church, or a spiritual or religious community or group. ____

I feel a sense of unity with things around me. ____

I trust my feelings more than my logical reasons. ____

I feel a spiritual connection with people. ____

I believe that miracles happen. ____

I have experiences that make my role in life clear. ____

I want to make the world a better place, like trying to prevent injustices. ____

SCORE-add your numbers _____

Please see the next page for your rating.

SCORE _____

40-50 = You are spiritually aware.
30-39 = You are as spiritually aware as many other people.
11-29 = You can learn more about spiritual life.
10 and under = You resist spiritual awareness.

Chapter 13

Behavior Change:
Find Your Humor And Fun

"Your sense of humor is one of the most powerful tools you
have to make certain that your daily mood and emotional
state support good health." Paul E. McGhee, Ph.D.

**Sense of humor is having the sense to know when to use humor
and when humor is being used**. There are healthy benefits to having a
good sense of humor and being able to laugh often, as children can do.

You can rate your sense of humor with some sources online. Use a
search engine like Google to find up-to-date quizzes. Type in *sense of
humor quiz* to search.

HelpGuide.org is a nonprofit guide to mental health and well-being.
The staff has ways to help you see the brighter side of life, and they have
given permission to use their ideas.

Laugh at yourself. Share your embarrassing moments. The best
way to take yourself less seriously is to talk about times when you took
yourself too seriously.

Attempt to laugh at situations rather than bemoan them. Look
for the humor in a bad situation, and uncover the irony and absurdity
of life. This will help improve your mood and the mood of those
around you.

Surround yourself with reminders to lighten up. Keep a toy on your desk or in your car. Put up a funny poster in your office. Choose a computer screensaver that makes you laugh. Frame photos of you and your family or friends having fun.

Keep things in perspective. Many things in life are beyond your control—particularly the behavior of other people. While you might think taking the weight of the world on your shoulders is admirable, in the long run it's unrealistic, unproductive, unhealthy, and even egotistical. Stress is a major impediment to humor and laughter.

Pay attention to children and emulate them. They are the experts on playing, taking life lightly, and laughing. Spend some time with them, and see how they use humor. It can be refreshing for a light-hearted approach.

Being able to laugh, play, and have fun makes life more enjoyable. When people can laugh together, it increases happiness and intimacy. Laughter also triggers healthy physical changes in the body. Humor and laughter strengthen your immune system, boost your energy, diminish pain, and protect you from the damaging effects of stress. "A good laugh recharges your battery." Unknown Author

LAUGHTER AS MEDICINE--It is said that young children laugh as much as 100 to 200 times a day, compared to a large majority of adults who only get zero to several daily laughs. Yet laughter is good not only for the body but also for the soul and spirit.

As adults, if we don't laugh as much as children do, we need to discover more ways to help us laugh. To motivate us to laugh more, here are some benefits of laughter I've discovered:

-Relaxes muscles throughout the body,
-Changes our perspective,
-Has positive benefits on mental functions,
-Reduces blood pressure and heart-rate, and
-It makes us feel good!

Studies show laughter can benefit the body in many ways:

~ Increases antibodies in saliva that combat upper respiratory infections,
~Secretes an enzyme that protects the stomach from forming ulcers,
~Reduces symptoms of neuralgia and rheumatism,
~Helps the body fight infection,
~Releases endorphins which provide natural pain relief,
~Tightens stomach muscles, and
~Helps move nutrients and oxygen to body tissues.

If you don't have a sense of humor, there's good news: you can develop one. It will help you communicate with others, and it can help you to not be so hard on yourself.

You can learn some jokes. Some people say they can never remember jokes, so find jokes that you really laugh at and memorize your favorites. Here are some of my favorites. Please share your favorites; send them to my Email: *sharonwpenn@gmail.com*

Jokes:

What children have learned:
***If you're gonna draw on the wall, do it behind the couch.
***Ask why until you understand.
***If you want a kitten, start out by asking for a horse.
***Making your bed is a waste of time.
***If your dog doesn't like somebody, you probably shouldn't either.
***Toads aren't ugly. They're just toads.
***Just keep banging until someone opens the door.
***Don't pop someone else's bubble.
***You shouldn't ask to start over just because you're losing the game.
***Chasing the cat is more fun than catching it.

More favorites:
***Sherlock Holmes and Dr. Watson went on a camping trip. After a good meal and a bottle of wine, they lay down for the night

and went to sleep. Some hours later, Holmes awoke and nudged his faithful friend.

"Watson, look up and tell me what you see."

Watson replied, "I see millions and millions of stars."

"And what does that tell you?" Holmes asked.

Watson pondered for a minute, "Astronomically, it tells me that there are millions of galaxies and potentially billions of planets. Astronomically I observe that Saturn is in Leo. Horologically, I deduce that the time is about a quarter past 3. Theologically, I see that God is all-powerful and that we are small and insignificant. Meteorologically, I suspect that we will have a beautiful day tomorrow. What does it tell *you*?"

Holmes was silent for a minute; then spoke, "Someone has stolen our tent."

***A middle-aged woman had a heart attack and was taken to the hospital, where she had a near-death experience. Seeing God, she asked, "Is my time up?"

"No," He replied. "You have another 40 years to live."

Upon recovery, the woman decided to stay in the hospital and have a facelift, liposuction and a tummy tuck. She even bleached her hair blond again, figuring that, as she had so many years left, she may as well make the most of them. After her release from the hospital, she was crossing the street on her way home when she was hit and killed by an ambulance. When she arrived in front of God, she complained: "I thought you said I had another 40 years! Why didn't you pull me out of the path of the ambulance?"

God replied, "I didn't recognize you."

***A little old man was driving down the freeway when his cell phone rang. It was his wife.

"Dear," she said, "I just heard on the radio that a car is going the wrong way on your highway. Please be careful!"

"It's not just one car," her husband replied. "There are hundreds of them!"

Some other favorites:

> ***The main reason Santa is so jolly is that he knows where all the bad girls live.

> ***I went to the bookstore and asked the saleswoman, "Where is the self-help section?" She said if she told me, it would defeat the purpose.

> ***What's the difference between a snowman and a snow woman? Snowballs.

> ***If man evolved from monkeys and apes, why do we still have monkeys and apes?

Just have to add a few lawyer jokes!

Jokes in Court:

> ***Lawyer: All your responses must be oral, OK? What school did you go to?
>
> Witness: Oral

> ***Lawyer: Doctor, do you recall the time that you examined the body?
>
> Witness: The autopsy started around 8 PM.
>
> Lawyer: And Mr. D was dead at the time?
>
> Witness: No, he was sitting on the table wondering why I was doing an autopsy.

> ***Lawyer: Doctor, before you performed the autopsy, did you check for a pulse?
>
> Witness: No.
>
> Lawyer: Did you check for blood pressure?
>
> Witness: No.
>
> Lawyer: Did you check for breathing?
>
> Witness: No.
>
> Lawyer: So, then it is possible that the patient was alive when you began the autopsy?
>
> Witness: No.

Lawyer: How can you be so sure, Doctor?

Witness: Because his brain was on my desk in a jar.

Lawyer: But could the patient have still been alive nevertheless?

Witness: Yes, it is possible that he could have been alive and practicing law somewhere.

A few more from children: A student was asked to list the 10 Commandments in any order. His answer: 3, 6, 1, 8, 4, 5, 9, 2, 10, 7.

> ***I was at the beach with my children when my four-year-old son ran up to me, grabbed my hand, and led me to the shore, where a seagull lay dead in the sand.
>
> "Mommy, what happened to him?" my son asked.
>
> "He died and went to heaven," I replied.
>
> My son thought a moment and then said, "And God threw him back down?"

And, more about *what children have learned*:

> ****No matter how hard you try, you can't baptize cats.*
>
> ****When your mom is mad at your dad, don't let her brush your hair.*
>
> ****If your sister hits you, don't hit her back. They always catch the second one.*
>
> ****You can't trust dogs to watch your food.*
>
> ****Don't sneeze when someone is cutting your hair.*
>
> ****Puppies still have bad breath even after eating a breath mint.*
>
> ****Never hold a vacuum cleaner and a cat at the same time.*

There's a connection between laughter and mental well-being. If you can laugh at something, then the seriousness is lessened.

Helpguide.org gives us some more help with humor:

~Laughter dissolves distressing emotions.

You can't feel anxious, angry, or sad when you're laughing.

~Laughter helps you relax and recharge. It reduces stress and increases energy, enabling you to stay focused and accomplish more.

-**Humor shifts perspective**, allowing you to see situations in a more realistic, less threatening light. A humorous perspective creates psychological distance, which can help you avoid feeling overwhelmed. Humor and playful communication strengthen our relationships by triggering positive feelings and fostering emotional connection. When we laugh with one another, a positive bond is created. This bond acts as a strong buffer against stress, disagreements, and disappointment.

> "There is a purifying power in laughter.
> It is truth in palatable form.
> It is instant vacation.
> Seeing the comical side of many situations
> makes life a great deal easier.
> It's like riding through life on sensitive springs that ease
> every jolt."
> Eugene P. Bertin 1968

CHECKLIST & CONTRACT

I WILL COMPLETE THIS CHECKLIST & CONTRACT FOR EACH BEHAVIOR I WORK ON.

____ I am motivated to change/improve my behavior:
Name Behavior: **Find my Humor and Fun**

____ I will begin by working to improve one behavior at a time.

____ I will complete this checklist for each behavior.

____ I will sign a contract and place it where I can see it often.

____ I will work with another person to improve this behavior.

____ I will keep a journal about my progress and feelings.

____ I will read Chapters 1 & 2.

____ I will complete the worksheets for Chapters 1 & 2.

____ I will read the chapter of the behavior I want to improve.

____ I will complete the worksheet(s) relevant to this chapter.

CONTRACT

As of today, I choose to improve my life, one behavior at a time, by **Finding My HUMOR AND FUN.**

Name_____ Date_____

Print and Post

Chapter 14

Behavior Change:
Help Yourself To Happiness

"It is not how much we have,
but how much we enjoy,
that makes happiness."
Charles Spurgeon

What is happiness? Some definitions I've found include Wikipedia's: Happiness is a mental or emotional state of well-being defined by positive or pleasant emotions ranging from contentment to intense joy.

William Gladstone said, "Be happy with what you have and are, be generous with both, and you won't have to hunt for happiness."

How do we get happy? Each person would report a different way they get to happiness, based on their life experiences as well as their attitude and the way they think about their situation.

How do we know when we are happy? We can ask ourselves what gives us satisfaction, pleasure, and a sense of fulfillment. If we can list some things under those categories, we are on our way to a definition of happiness and contentment for ourselves. Some people know when they are feeling content with their life and don't feel they need anything else.

Mental health practitioners study happy people and have come up with behaviors they believe can show what makes a person happy. They say our psychological well-being is affected by three main factors:

our genetic makeup, our environment, as well as our thoughts and actions or life skills. We can't do anything about the genetic makeup, but we certainly can do something about our environment and our thoughts and actions.

This chapter will address the things we can change if we believe we could be happier. We will start with what gives us satisfaction, pleasure, and a sense of fulfillment. When you take the happiness assessment located at the end of this chapter and in the Workbook Section, you will see the areas you are happy with and the areas in which you believe you are deficient. You can go from there and start filling your *happiness* basket by picking the one you want to work on first. Remember: pick just one at a time. When that one is filled, go on to the next.

I have created a Happiness DOs and DON'Ts list. You can print it as a poster to put on your fridge, bulletin board, or put in a frame to remind you and others of some of the ways to get or keep happiness around you. The poster is at the end of the chapter.

Penn's DOs and DON'Ts for Happiness

DO smile. Do this first. If you don't feel like smiling, do it anyway, and continue smiling until you really want to smile. FAKE it 'til you MAKE it. It will happen. I use the "As If" theory—act *as if* you're loving life and then you will.

DO think and express gratitude. Think now about something you are grateful for, and if it involves someone else, tell them. Tell them now by calling, texting, or emailing them. You can also put it on social media so everyone can benefit.

DO keep a gratitude journal along with a diary of daily living and special occasions. It will be a wonderful way to give you and your family memories of times gone by. It's also an excellent way to get you to focus on your many blessings.

DO a good deed. Think about a person who can use your help, or someone you want to repay for doing a good deed for you. Maybe it's a neighbor or friend who is struggling and can use a gesture of friendship. Let them know you are there for them: to talk, to pick up items from the store, to babysit or pet sit, or anything they may need at this time. Take them a food item you've cooked or purchased at a specialty store, or flowers from your garden or a nearby florist.

DO stay in touch with family and friends. More and more we hear how important it is to have social connections for a healthy and happy life. Sometimes it's hard to stop in your busy life to telephone your parents or that elderly aunt, visit a neighbor, or call your sister or brother who is probably as busy as you are. Find ways to remind yourself to do this because you know how important it is.

DO notice other happy people. What works for them to stay on top of the world? If it's not readily apparent, ask them. They'll probably love to tell you. Then try those things. If you've gotten a number of things, try only one at a time and stay focused until it's a habit, then go to the next one.

DO expand your happiness portfolio. In addition to writing down what makes you happy, also write down your bucket list—things you plan to do or want to do in this life. Then, take action and start doing one right now!

DO create your own group. Know that you are a social person and need a sense of belonging. If there's not a group of people you can join, create one. What are your interests? For example, if it's writing and you can't find a group, start one yourself. I've done this, and it was so much fun. Since all the group members were going away for the summer, we wrote a mystery novella, named *A Royal Mystery*, (we lived in a community called Royal Highlands). Each person wrote a chapter of the book. We went alphabetically by the last name; and, luckily, the first person, Mimi B., was an excellent writer and set the tone of the book.

We all had computers, so as we wrote our chapter, we would send it to the others. Then the next chapter would be written and sent until the mystery was solved by the final writer. This kept us connected through the summer, and we had a great time writing it. I still have a copy and re-read it once in a while—another way to hold on to memories.

If you create your own group, you'll be amazed to find there are so many people out there who have your same interests but haven't done anything about it. So you're not just helping yourself to happiness but others benefit, also.

If you like needlework or quilting, Bible study, playing cards or mahjong, exercise, reading, gardening, or sports, etc., you can find or start a group. It can begin with one or two other people, and expand when more people hear about it. Start a walking or exercise group in your neighborhood and you may find other things you'd like to do together.

DO consider Meetup Groups. Check out the meetup groups online; there are many, and there's probably one near you that shares your interest. You can start here: *www.meetup.com*. The groups are divided by interests; when you click on a group you're interested in, you can then see where the closest meetup will be. It will be more fun if you get a friend to join you.

DO volunteer to help out at one of the many places asking for assistance. Your local library may have lists of places that need your help. Or you may want to help out at a school where your child, grandchild, or neighbor's child attends. You may know someone in a nursing home you can visit and then help others who don't get visitors.

DO consider pets. Do you have a pet already? Some people don't have pets for various reasons: they travel in their retirement years or others spend many hours at work, or they aren't allowed to have pets where they live, or someone they live with doesn't like pets or has pet allergies. If you like pets and want to get one, you'll find a way to overcome any obstacle. Sometimes your pet really can be your best friend, and that's good therapy. When you play with them, you take your mind off your problems. And when you take care of them, you're focused on something outside yourself, which can be therapeutic.

DON'T allow negativity to rule your life. Move forward. What can help remind you of the positives in your life? Maybe it's photos of your favorite people, pets, or activities. It could be your accomplishments and awards. Do you have favorite quotes or inspirational sayings that pump you up when you are down? See Chapter 15 if you need quotes. Keep reminders near you of all the things that help lift your spirits when you are down or feeling negative.

DON'T dwell on the past. Live in the now and leave the past behind, where it belongs. Maybe you had a poor childhood and the memories of it haunt you. Do you really want it to continue to control your life? Let it go; you can't change the past but you can control the present. When it comes up in your memory, tell yourself, "That will no longer affect me and I'm letting it go to live a joyful life." Say it to yourself as many times as you need until it goes away.

DON'T live with regrets. Maybe you wish you had done some things in years past. If it's not too late and it will add happiness, go for it! Perhaps you did things you now wish never happened. If you can make amends, do it. Did you hurt someone and need to apologize? Maybe it's been years; that won't matter when you tell the offended person, "I'm sorry." You can try to see them face-to-face but if necessary, call, write, email, or text. Just do it now!

If the person is gone—either died or nowhere to be found, what can you do to rectify the situation? Maybe a memorial if they've died or a donation to a charity in their name if you can't find them. Let me know if you have any other ideas and I will share with readers on my website. Thank you. *Email me: sharonwpenn@gmail.com*

As we age and have losses in our life, i.e., loved ones, physical health, and dreams, we feel grief and have to rely on other factors to create our contentment. It can be the memories of those years with our spouse, children, and other loved ones (extended family and friends). Having photographs of day-to-day activities and special occasions, showing the happy faces of people in your life, can build on your memories of the moments with them. Keeping journals and scrapbooks through the years is another way to help one jog the memories of past years.

Another fun way to help keep memories alive is to videotape or audiotape reunions with your people where you sit together and talk about your memories of times gone by. Using mementos and photographs can jog everyone's memories as you sit together for these sessions. Think about scheduling one of these meetings soon. You'll enjoy it while it's being recorded and, again, when you watch it.

Start by picking one thing you want to do; begin it now. Then, when you're ready—no rush—pick another. Before you know it, your life will be so full you'll wonder that you ever had too much free time.

If you haven't already, please complete the Habits of Happy People Checklist. It will give you ideas of ways to create your own happy habits. Please see at the end of this chapter and in the Worksheet Section.

"In our daily lives, we must see that it is not happiness
that makes us grateful,
But gratefulness that makes us happy."
Brother David Steindl-Rast

STOP now and name three things you are grateful for
and notice how much better you feel.

POSTER
HELP YOURSELF to HAPPINESS
Penn's DOs and DON'Ts

~DO SMILE.

~DO THINK & EXPRESS GRATITUDE.

~ DO KEEP A GRATITUDE JOURNAL.

~DO EXPAND YOUR HAPPINESS PORTFOLIO.

~DO A GOOD DEED.

~DO STAY CLOSE with FAMILY and FRIENDS.

~DO NOTICE OTHER HAPPY PEOPLE.

~DON'T ALLOW NEGATIVITY TO RULE YOUR LIFE.

~DON'T DWELL ON THE PAST.

~DON'T PUT YOURSELF DOWN.

~DON'T FORGET-only one at a time.

Print and post where you and others will see it.

CHECKLIST & CONTRACT

I WILL COMPLETE THIS CHECKLIST & CONTRACT FOR EACH BEHAVIOR I WORK ON.

_____ I am motivated to change/improve my behavior:
Name Behavior: **Help Myself to HAPPINESS**

_____ I will begin by working to improve one behavior at a time.

_____ I will complete this checklist for each behavior.

_____ I will sign a contract and place it where I can see it often.

_____ I will work with another person to improve this behavior.

_____ I will keep a journal about my progress and feelings.

_____ I will read Chapters 1 & 2.

_____ I will complete the worksheets for Chapters 1 & 2.

_____ I will read the chapter of the behavior I want to improve.

_____ I will complete the worksheet(s) relevant to this chapter.

CONTRACT

As of today, I choose to improve my life, one behavior at a time, by **Helping Myself to Happiness.**

Name_____ Date_____

Print and Post

WORKSHEET 14

HABITS OF HAPPY PEOPLE

Use the scale below to answer the 12 questions,
based on the past month.

N=Never   *R=Rarely*   *S=Sometimes*
       O=Often   *M=Most of the time*

1-Do you have feelings of gratitude toward people and events from your past and present? _____

2-Do you feel your life has purpose? _____

3-Are you optimistic about the future? _____

4-Are you able to focus on the present moment and not get distracted by thoughts of the past or future? _____

5-Do you share your feelings with friends or relatives? _____

6-Do you practice at least 5-20 min. of daily physical exercise? _____

7-Do you have a pet or pets to take care of? _____

8-Do you offer to help out a friend, neighbor, a co-worker (babysit, cook a meal, drive them someplace, accompany them as support, etc.)? _____

9-Do you tell people you are grateful for what they do for you, or what they have done for you in the past? _____

10-Do you engage in activities you find challenging and absorbing (sports, writing, taking classes, gardening, attending a book club or other type club, etc.)? _____

11-Do you participate in a church, spiritual community, or group? _____

12-Do you volunteer with a group that asks for help (hospital, school, nursing home, homeless shelter, animal shelter, etc.)? _____

SCORING:

You are probably satisfied with your life if you answered *Often* or *Most of the Time* on five or more questions,

If fewer than five, look at the items you reported *Never* or *Rarely* and decide now to do one of these at a time. Then, when it becomes a habit, you can respond: *Often* or *Most of the Time.*

Notice numbers 5-12 are *action* questions. If you do these first, you may see numbers 1-4 change to *Often.*

Sharon W. Penn –Change 1 Behavior; Improve Your Life 2017
Email me: sharonwpenn@gmail.com

Chapter 15

QUOTES and Other Thoughts

I have used quotes throughout this book, and in case you only pick certain chapters to read, I have put all the quotes in this last chapter. You may be as inspired as I am when you read quotes from other people, so I don't want you to miss any of them.

Also, I have inspirational quotes posted in different parts of my house that I have been collecting for many years, and I want to share those with you. I hope they are as helpful to you as they are to me.

Quotes From This Book:

In the Introduction:

"To exist is to change, To change is to mature, To mature is to go on creating oneself endlessly."
Henri Bergson

"Change occurs through relearning, restructuring, redefining old, used, or even abused behaviors, thoughts, and feelings that progress from bad to good, unhealthy to healthy, from negative to positive positions."
Margaret Click, Ph.D.

"When you change the way you look at things,
the things you look at change."
Wayne Dyer, Ph.D.

"Never doubt that a small group of thoughtful, committed
people can change the world. Indeed, it is the only thing
that ever has."
Margaret Mead

IMPROVEMENT: "The joy of life is living it, or so it seems to me;
In finding shackles on your wrists, then struggling till you're free;
In seeing wrongs and righting them, in dreaming splendid dreams,
Then toiling till the vision is as real as moving streams.
The happiest mortal on the earth is he who ends his day
By leaving better than he found to bloom along the way..."
Edgar Albert Guest - *b. 1881, d. 1959*

Chapter 1: *Mentally Healthy People*

"As a single footstep will not make a path on the earth, so
a single thought will not make a pathway in the mind. To
make a deep physical path, we walk again and again. To
make a deep mental path, we must think over and over the
kind of thoughts we wish to dominate our lives."
H. David Thoreau

Chapter 2: *Why It's Hard To Change a Habit*

"The things which are impossible with man are possible
with God."
(Luke 18:27)

"Whatever you can do or dream you can do, begin it,
Boldness has genius, power, and magic in it."
Goethe

Chapter 3: Are You Addicted?

"We may think there is willpower involved, but more likely... change is due to want power. Wanting the new addiction more than the old one. Wanting the new me in preference to the person I am now."
George A. Sheehan

Chapter 4: *Convey Your Approachability:*

"A SMILE costs nothing but gives much. It enriches those who receive, without making poorer those who give…"
Unknown Author

"For human beings, you need two hugs a day to survive, four hugs for maintenance, six hugs to grow." Virginia Satir

Chapter 5: *Boost Your Self-Esteem*

"Never forget that you are one of a kind. And never forget, no matter how overwhelming life's challenges and problems seem to be, that one person can make a difference in the world. In fact, it is always because of one person that all changes that matter in the world. So be that one person." Buckminster Fuller

"It is easy to feel worthy and good about ourselves when things are going well. The trick is to have the seeds of the positive self-love, self-image, and self-awareness so deeply planted and well-fertilized within us that we feel worthy, compassionate, and loving toward ourselves even when, and especially when events are not going well."
Margaret Click, Ph.D.

"Whether you think you can or you think you can't, you're right."
Henry Ford

Chapter 6: *The Blues Busters*

"If you always do what you've always done, you'll always
get what you've always gotten."
Jessie Potter

Chapter 7: Manage Your Anger

"If you are patient in one moment of anger, you will escape
a hundred days of sorrow." Chinese Proverb

Chapter 8: *Enhance Your Personal Relationship*

"Do nothing from selfishness or empty conceit, but with
humility of mind let each of you regard one another as
more important than himself; do not merely look out for
your own personal interests, but also for the interests of
others."
Philippians 2:3-4

"A smile, a head nod, even just grunting to show you're
listening to your partner—those are all positive."
Dr. John Gottman

"In any interaction, we have the opportunity to connect
with our partner or to turn away. If we consistently turn
away, then over time the foundation of the marriage
(relationship) can slowly erode."
Dr. John Gottman

Chapter 10: *Treasure Your Relationships*

"One of the most beautiful qualities of true friendship is to
understand and to be understood."
Seneca

"A true friend (discloses) freely, advises justly, assists readily, adventures boldly, takes all patiently, defends courageously, and continues a friend unchangeably."
William Penn

"He that has once done you a kindness will be more ready to do you another than he whom you yourself have obliged."
Benjamin Franklin

Chapter 11: *Choose to Age Gracefully*

"There is a fountain of youth: it is your mind, your talents, the creativity you bring to your life and the lives of people you love. When you learn to tap this source, you will truly have defeated age."
Sophia Loren

"Everything can be taken from a man but one thing: the last of the human freedoms—to choose one's attitude in any given set of circumstances, to choose one's own way."
Viktor Frankl

"The remarkable thing is, we have a choice every day regarding the attitude we will embrace for that day."
Charles Swindoll

"We cannot change the fact that people will act in a certain way. We cannot change the inevitable. The only thing we can do is play on the one string we have…That is our attitude. I am convinced that life is 10% what happens to me and 90% how I react to it. And so it is with you… We are in charge of our attitude." Charles Swindoll

"A healthy attitude is contagious but don't wait to catch it from others. Be a carrier."
Tom Stoppard

Chapter 12: *Seek Your Spirituality*

"Just as a candle cannot burn without fire, man cannot live without a spiritual life." Buddha

"The essential lesson I've learned in life is to just be yourself. Treasure the magnificent being that you are and recognize first and foremost you're not here as a human being only. You're a spiritual being having a human experience."
Wayne Dyer, Ph.D.

"The fact that I can plant a seed and it becomes a flower, share a bit of knowledge and it becomes another's, smile at someone and receive a smile in return, are to me continual spiritual exercises."
Leo Buscaglia, Ph.D.

Chapter 13: *Find Your Humor and Fun*

"Your sense of humor is one of the most powerful tools you have to make certain that your daily mood and emotional state support good health."
Paul E. McGhee, Ph.D.

"There is a purifying power in laughter. It is truth in palatable form. It is instant vacation. Seeing the comical side of many situations makes life a great deal easier. It's like riding through life on sensitive springs that ease every jolt."
Eugene P. Bertin 1968

Chapter 14: *Help Yourself to Happiness*

"It is not how much we have,
but how much we enjoy,
that makes happiness."
Charles Spurgeon

"Be happy with what you have and are, be generous
with both, and you won't have to hunt for happiness."
William Gladstone

~~~

"In our daily lives, we must see that it is not happiness that
makes us grateful,
But gratefulness that makes us happy."
Br. David Steindl-Rast

"STOP now and name three things you are grateful for
And notice how much better You feel."

~~~

Quotes and Thoughts
From the Front of My Refrigerator:

ON THIS DAY…Mend a quarrel. Search out a forgotten
friend. Dismiss suspicion, and replace it with trust. Write
a love letter. Share some treasure. Give a soft answer.
Encourage youth. Manifest your loyalty in a word or
deed. Keep a promise. Find the time. Forego a grudge.
Forgive an enemy. Listen. Apologize if you were wrong.
Try to understand. Flout envy. Examine your demands on
others. Think first of someone else. Appreciate, be kind,
be gentle. Laugh a little more. Deserve confidence. Take
up arms against malice. Decry complacency. Express
your gratitude. Worship your God. Gladden the heart of
a child. Take pleasure in the beauty and wonder of the
earth. Speak your love. Speak it again. Speak it still again.
Speak it still once again.

~~~

If you don't love it, use it, wear it, or have room for it, it's clutter.
Keep—Give away—Throw Away—Recycle.
Schedule 1 - 2 hours to start to de-clutter.
Make 4 piles; get rid of 3.
If not sure, keep item one month,
then get rid of if you haven't used it.

~~~

NO FOOD TASTES AS GOOD AS BEING THIN FEELS.

~~~

MEDICAL INFORMATION
Do this to help lower blood pressure and diabetes:
Mix together—1-quart grape juice, 1-pint apple juice,
¼ cup raw honey, ¾ cup apple cider vinegar.
Drink 2 ounces on an empty stomach every morning.

~~~

TEST YOURSELF
Forget the chest-clutching you've seen in the movies. Heart attacks can affect people
very differently, and the signs may be particularly subtle in women.

Which of these may be a heart attack sign?
- Pain in the shoulder, neck, jaw, or upper back
- Dizziness, lightheadedness, or fainting
- A feeling of "doom" that doesn't go away
- Shortness of breath
- Pressure or pain in the chest, often on the left side
- Nausea and vomiting
- Sudden sweating
- Extreme fatigue

ANSWER: All of them

MEMORIZE THESE NUMBERS--You want to be below:
100—Blood Sugar **120/80**—Blood Pressure
200—Total Cholesterol

5 WAYS TO PROTECT YOUR HEART

Fill your plate with colorful fruits and veggies.
Eat a handful of nuts.
Avoid fats, fried foods, baked goods, and sugary drinks.
Wear a fitness monitor and aim for 10,000 steps daily.
Distance yourself from secondhand smoke.

~~~

STROKE WARNING SIGNS / THINK F.A.S.T.

F=Facial Droop – Have person smile. If smile droops down on one side, it may be a stroke.
A=Arm Drift - Have person hold both arms out even with their eyes.
S=Speech – Have person repeat a phrase like "you can't teach an old dog new tricks." If speech is slurred, absent or abnormal, it may be a stroke.
T=Time – Call 911 immediately if the person fails one or more of these tests, because they may be having a stroke.

~~~

HEART ATTACK WARNING SIGNS

Chest discomfort such as a tight pressure, fullness or squeezing in the center of your chest, often lasting more than a few minutes and may go away and then return.

- Tingling or Pain in the jaw, left shoulder blade, back, arm or throat
- Cold sweats, paleness or clammy skin
- Nausea or vomiting
- Dizziness or lightheadedness
- Fatigue   Florida Hospital Newsletter 2015

DIABETES HEART ATTACK WARNING SIGNS

- Mild chest pain
- Sudden onset of shortness of breath
- Unexplained high blood sugars

If you are experiencing any of the symptoms above, contact
911 immediately. Florida Hospital Newsletter 2015

From My Office Bulletin Boards:

"REMEMBER the THREE R's
Respect for self;
Respect for others; and
Responsibility for all your actions."

~~~

**"The person who removes a mountain begins by
carrying away small stones."
Confucius**

~~~

"Frame every so-called disaster with these words:
In five years, will this matter?"

~~~

"However good or bad a situation is, it will change."

~~~

"Get outside every day.
Miracles are waiting everywhere."
Regina Brett

~~~

"No matter how you feel, get up, dress up, and show up."
Regina Brett

~~~

"If you always do what you've always done, you'll
always get what you've always gotten."
Jessie Potter

~~~

TO LIVE A GOOD LIFE
"Be thankful for what you have.
Share what you have with others.
Find the good in people and tell them.
Smile often.
Show gratitude.
Accomplish something good every day."

~~~

"Growing older means realizing that our life is what our thoughts make of it."

~~~

"Change to positive life-energizing thoughts and you change your world."

~~~

"Happiness is a decision."
Henrik Edberg

~~~

How to Have a Lovely Day:
"Smile
Slow down
Say thank you
Give lots of compliments
Dress nicely
Observe and listen
Be charming
Laugh lots
Wish others a lovely day"

~~~

"HOPE is the thing with feathers
That perches in the soul
And sings the tune
Without the words
And never stops at all."
Emily Dickinson

~ ~ ~

"Some rich people stay rich by living like they're broke;
Some broke people stay broke by living like they're rich."

~ ~ ~

"We live on a blue planet that circles around a ball of fire;
Next to a moon that moves the sea, and
You don't believe in miracles?"

~ ~ ~

**"Accept what is, let go of what was,
And have faith in what will be."**
David Wolfe

~ ~ ~

**"So much of life depends on our attitude.
The way we choose to see things, and respond
to others makes all the difference.
To do the best we can and then choose to be happy about
our circumstances, whatever they may be,
Can bring peace and contentment.
We can't direct the wind, but we can adjust the sails."
Thomas S. Monson**

~ ~ ~

**"Whatever you can do, or dream you can do,
Begin it,
Boldness has genius, power, and magic in it."**
Goethe

~ ~ ~

"Singing daily for 10 minutes: Reduces stress, clears sinuses,
improves posture, and can help you live longer."

"Unless you're tone-deaf, in which case
(for the sake of people nearby),
Listen to the Beatles and Lip-sync!"

~ ~ ~

"Get rid of anything that isn't useful, beautiful, or joyful."

~ ~ ~

**"Want to keep CHRIST in CHRISTMAS?
Feed the hungry
Clothe the naked
Forgive the guilty
Welcome the stranger and the unwanted child
Care for the ill and elderly
Love your enemy."**

~ ~ ~

A PARTING THOUGHT:

Success

"To laugh often and much;
To win the respect of intelligent people
and the affection of children;

To earn the appreciation of honest critics
and endure the betrayal of false friends;

To appreciate beauty, to find the best in others;

To leave the world a bit better, whether by a
healthy child, a garden patch, or a redeemed
social condition;

To know even one life has breathed easier
because you have lived.

This is to have succeeded."

Ralph Waldo Emerson (1803 - 1882)
American Essayist & Poet

WORKSHEET SECTION

WORKSHEET 1

RATE YOUR MENTAL WELL-BEING

Please read Chapter 1: Mentally Healthy People.

Please Note: *This test is designed for adults. Adolescent self-images are still forming; therefore, this assessment will not be accurate for them.*

Please use this scale to respond:

Never=1   Rarely=2   Sometimes=3
Often=4   Most of the time=5

1-I have positive relationships with others. _____

2-I have a positive evaluation of myself. _____

3-I believe I control my life. _____

4-I think my life has purpose and meaning. _____

5-I have a balance of positive and negative emotions with work, family, and social life. _____

6-I manage my world pretty well. _____

7-I cope with stress. _____

8- I have a handle on how my family traits affect me. _____

9-I cope with adversity. _____

10-My family, friends, co-workers, neighbors, and others are there for me when I need them. _____

11-I work on staying healthy. _____

12-I do some form of physical activity several times a week—gardening, aerobics, walking, stretching, swimming, workout at a gym or home, dancing, weight-lifting, etc. _____

13-I practice relaxation techniques—meditation, music, television, yoga, reading, etc. _____

14-I have a spiritual life—prayer, bible study, church attendance, meditation, or other. _____

15-I work at continuing my personal growth and improving my life. _____

Add your numbers: Never ____ Rarely ____ Sometimes ____ Often ____ Most of the time ____ TOTAL _____

SCORING:
- If you scored 51-75, you have an extremely healthy mental well-being.
- If you scored 41-50, your score is average which is normal.
- If you scored 40 or less, your mental well-being can use some work.
- The good news is that you can improve your mental well-being. Notice where you answered *Never, Rarely, or Sometimes* to determine which behaviors you can start to work on, then check out Chapters 4 - 14 in the book for behaviors to change. Work on changing only one behavior at a time.
- Please consider seeing a mental health professional if your score is below 30.

Date_____   CHANGE 1 BEHAVIOR; IMPROVE YOUR LIFE
Sharon W. Penn 2017   Email me: *sharonwpenn@gmail.com*

WORKSHEET 2

STEPS TO CHANGE A HABIT

Please read Chapter 2—Why It's Hard to Change a Habit

10 STEPS TO CHANGE A HABIT   **Do It Now;**
                                                 Write It Here

1-Clearly define the habit you want to change---
Example: Lose 10 pounds in five weeks.

2-Define how you will meet your goal---
Example: Choose a favorite diet plan.

3-Make the goal measurable---How many times?
Example: Perform the diet plan five days weekly.

4-Divide tasks into small, short-term sub-goals ---
Example: Lose two pounds weekly.

5-Identify replacement actions---
Example: Instead of snacking, go for a walk, call a friend, etc.

6-Write it down---Put it on paper—the goal, tasks to meet the goal,
replacement actions, affirmations, etc. Write on 3x5 cards.

7-Choose an advisor---
Example: A support group, mentor, friend, diet buddy, fitness expert, or other.

8-Use affirmations and visualizations --- Change your thoughts,
which change attitudes, which change actions—Say it & See it.
Example: "Each day my body becomes smaller and firmer."

9-Begin today. Put date here

10-Keep a journal. Write down changes and progress you see.

Date_____   CHANGE 1 BEHAVIOR; IMPROVE YOUR LIFE
Sharon W. Penn 2017   Email me: *sharonwpenn@gmail.com*

WORKSHEET 3

Please read Chapter 3—Are You Addicted?

The following test rates your addiction (or not) to alcohol:

The AUDIT Test for Alcohol Addiction (Alcoholism) *Alcohol Use Disorders Identification Test) (10 questions) was developed by the World Health Organization (WHO). The test correctly classifies 95% of people into either alcoholics or non-alcoholics. An updated version is available to take online at www.who.org.*

To correctly answer some of these questions you need to know the definition of a drink. For this test one drink is:
One can of beer (12 oz or approx 330 ml of 5% alcohol), or
One glass of wine (5 oz or approx 140 ml of 12% alcohol), or
One shot of liquor (1.5 oz or approx 40 ml of 40% alcohol).

__1. How often do you have a drink containing alcohol?
Never (score 0)
Monthly or Less (score 1)
2-4 times a month (score 2)
2-3 times a week (score 3)
4 or more times a week (score 4)

__2. How many alcoholic drinks do you have on a typical day when you are drinking?
1 or 2 (0)
3 or 4 (1)
5 or 6 (2)
7-9 (3)
10 or more (4)

__3. How often do you have 6 or more drinks on one occasion?
Never (0)
Less than monthly (1)
Monthly (2)
Weekly (3)
Daily or almost daily (4)

___4. How often during the past year have you found that you drank more or for a longer time than you intended?
Never (0)
Less than monthly (1)
Monthly (2)
Weekly (3)
Daily or almost daily (4)

___5. How often during the past year have you failed to do what was normally expected of you because of your drinking?
Never (0)
Less than monthly (1)
Monthly (2)
Weekly (3)
Daily or almost daily (4)

___6. How often during the past year have you had a drink in the morning to get yourself going after a heavy drinking session?
Never (0)
Less than monthly (1)
Monthly (2)
Weekly (3)
Daily or almost daily (4)

___7. How often during the past year have you felt guilty or remorseful after drinking?
Never (0)
Less than monthly (1)
Monthly (2)
Weekly (3)
Daily or almost daily (4)

___8. How often during the past year have you been unable to remember what happened the night before because of your drinking?
Never (0)
Less than monthly (1)
Monthly (2)
Weekly (3)
Daily or almost daily (4)

__9. Have you or anyone else been injured as a result of your drinking?
No (0)
Yes, but not in the past year (2)
Yes, during the past year (4)

__10. Has a relative, friend, doctor, or health care worker been concerned about your drinking, or suggested that you cut down?
No (0)
Yes, but not in the past year (2)
Yes, during the past year (4)

Your score:
If you scored 8-10 or more, you are probably addicted to alcohol.

NOTE: It may seem like the AUDIT questionnaire is an easy test to fail. If you applied this test to other aspects of your life you will almost certainly come up as being addicted to something. For example, most people watch too much television or eat too much of their favorite food. But those are so-called "soft addictions" and the AUDIT questionnaire was not designed to assess them. It is extremely reliable when it comes to assessing alcohol addiction. (The pdf format version of the AUDIT is available through the WHO Email. Copyright 1993 World Health Organization.)   Babor

WORKSHEET 4

APPROACHABILITY CHECKLIST

Please read Chapter 4—Convey Your Approachability.

7 TASKS-1 a day   TIMES TRIED 2-10 X daily

1-Smile Appropriately ---

2-Eye Contact ---

3-Greet/Get Response ---

4-Touch Appropriately ---

5-Use Open Body Language ---

6-Compliment People ---

7-Say Name in Conversation ---

Please use my email to tell me about your experiences.

Date_____   CHANGE 1 BEHAVIOR; IMPROVE YOUR LIFE
Sharon W. Penn 2017   Email me: *sharonwpenn@gmail.com*

Please start out by doing one of these behaviors, one at a time with 2-10 people, until it becomes a habit. Then, go to another behavior until it becomes a habit. Soon, you will have mastered all of them. Please tell me about your experiences. Email me: sharonwpenn@gmail.com

WORKSHEET 5A

SELF-ESTEEM SURVEY

Please read Chapter 5: Boost Your Self-Esteem.

Please respond to the questions using the following scale:

Never=1 **Rarely=2** **Sometimes=3**
Often=4 **Most of the time=5**

Do you make eye contact with others? ____

Do you volunteer to help needy people? ____

Are you honest with your feelings when dealing with others? ____

Did you feel loved as a child? ____

Do you feel loved now? ____

Do you avoid smoking or overeating? ____

Do you avoid abusing alcohol or drugs? ____

Are you free of colds, flu, and other illnesses? ____

Do you choose not to be angry? ____

If you do become angry, do you tell the person how you feel in a non-threatening way? ____

Do you speak your mind when an issue comes up about which you have strong feelings? ____

Do you avoid telling lies or half-truths? ____

Do you take risks? ____

Are you compassionate of others? ____

TOTAL YOUR POINTS _____

YOUR TOTAL POINTS _____

If your total points for the Self-Esteem Survey are:

50-70 – You have excellent self-esteem.

42-49 - Good; can use some work.

41 and below - Work on building your self-esteem by reading and practicing the habits in Chapter 5.

Date_____

Sharon W. Penn 2017

CHANGE 1 BEHAVIOR; IMPROVE YOUR LIFE

Email me: *sharonwpenn@gmail.com*

WORKSHEET 5B

SELF-ESTEEM REVIEW

Please read Chapter 5: Boost Your Self-Esteem.

Please make copies so you can do the rating often. You can use this as a progress report. Answer the statements once a week, and later, once a month to see how your self-esteem is changing as you make behavior changes. Keep the worksheets in a folder or on your computer.

How My Self-Esteem is NOW:

- Things I Do Well:

- Positive Ways I Share Feelings:

- Skills I Have:

- Talents I Have:

- Ways I'm Learning to Take Care of Myself:

- Ways I'm Making Positive Changes:

- Personal Characteristics that Help Me to Grow and Change:

Date_____   CHANGE 1 BEHAVIOR; IMPROVE YOUR LIFE
Sharon W. Penn 2017   Email me: *sharonwpenn@gmail.com*

WORKSHEET 6A

DEPRESSION SCALE

Please read Chapter 6: Try the Blues Busters.

Please use this scale to respond for how you have felt during the past two weeks:

Never=1   **Rarely=2**   **Sometimes=3**
Often=4   **Most of the time=5**

I have a poor appetite or I overeat. ____

I have insomnia or I oversleep. ____

I have low energy or fatigue. ____

I have low self-esteem. ____

I have poor concentration. ____

I have difficulty making decisions. ____

I have feelings of hopelessness. ____

I have little interest or pleasure in anything. ____

I feel depressed. ____

I feel suicidal. ____ Total Score _____

If your score is 40 or more; or if you feel suicidal or depressed for most of the day, more days than not, please see a mental health provider or your medical doctor NOW.

MENTAL HEALTH CRISIS HOTLINE
1-800-553-4539 or 1-888-269-4389

If you feel suicidal, or if you have five or more of the other nine symptoms on this Depression Scale during the same 2-week period; and at least one of the symptoms is either depressed mood or loss of interest or pleasure, please seek professional help, now. DSM-5

Depression (major depressive disorder) is a common and serious medical illness that negatively affects how you feel, the way you think and how you act. Fortunately, it is also treatable. Depression causes feelings of sadness and/or a loss of interest in activities once enjoyed. It can lead to a variety of emotional and physical problems and can decrease a person's ability to function at work and home. DSM-5

Date_____   CHANGE 1 BEHAVIOR; IMPROVE YOUR LIFE
Sharon W. Penn 2017   Email me: *sharonwpenn@gmail.com*

WORKSHEET 6B

BLUES BUSTERS CHECKLIST

Please read Chapter 6--Try the Blues Busters.

Choose one each day until it becomes a habit:

Daily Task   Times Tried

1-Take a walk, exercise, or do yoga…

2-Schedule a social event…

3-Have close, loving relationships…

4-Create successes for yourself…

5-Help someone in need…

6-Treat yourself to pleasures…

7-Get out your coloring book…

8-EVERY DAY: express appreciation…

9-EVERY DAY: write in a gratitude journal…

10-EVERY DAY: pray & meditate…

11-EVERY DAY: take one step at a time…

Date_____   CHANGE 1 BEHAVIOR; IMPROVE YOUR LIFE
Sharon W. Penn 2017   Email me: *sharonwpenn@gmail.com*

WORKSHEET 7A

ANGER RATING SCALE

Please read Chapter 7: Manage Your Anger.

Read the statements, and then write the appropriate number by it to indicate how you feel most of the time, or for the past weeks.

Never=1   **Rarely=2**   **Sometimes=3**
Often=4   **Most of the time=5**

I hold on to angry feelings. _____

I get angry with my family. _____

I am known as a hot-headed person. _____

I get angry at other drivers when I am driving. _____

I feel anger when I am not praised for doing good work. _____

I get angry with co-workers and salespeople. _____

I say nasty things when I am angry. _____

I feel anger when I am falsely accused. _____

When I get frustrated, I feel like hitting someone. _____

I show my temper by yelling at others. _____

ADD YOUR NUMBERS _____

Scoring is on the next page.

SCORING:

If you scored below 29, you are among the least angry people.

If you scored 30-39, your anger level is about average.

If you scored 40 or more, your anger level is higher than most people.

You can work on lowering your anger level by reading and practicing the habits in Manage Your Anger, Chapter 7.

If you have anger management issues, print and post PENN'S ANGER CONTROL DOs & DON"Ts in Chapter 7. View them often, commit them to memory, and work on the behaviors, one at a time, until it becomes a habit.

If you need additional help, please see a mental health provider, or call: 1-800-553-4539 or 1-888-269-4389.

Date_____   CHANGE 1 BEHAVIOR; IMPROVE YOUR LIFE
Sharon W. Penn 2017   Email me: *sharonwpenn@gmail.com*

WORKSHEET 7B

MANAGE YOUR ANGER

Please read Chapter 7: Manage Your Anger.

Use 7 Easy-to-Follow Anger Management Tips.
Choose one behavior at a time until it becomes a habit.

When you're angry, do this:

Daily Tasks   Times Tried

1-Think before you speak;
once you're calm,
express your anger---

2-Stick with 'I' statements---

3-Get some exercise---

4-Take a timeout when angry---

5-Identify possible solutions---

6-Use humor to release tension---

7-Practice relaxation skills---

If you believe you need more help controlling your anger than you have in this chapter, please contact a mental health provider. Help is available.
Call: **1-800-553-4539 or 1-888-269-4389.**

Date_____   CHANGE 1 BEHAVIOR; IMPROVE YOUR LIFE
Sharon W. Penn 2017   Email me: *sharonwpenn@gmail.com*

WORKSHEET 8

RELATIONSHIP REVIEW for COUPLES
Please read Chapter 8--Enhance Your Relationship.

1~ Describe the relationship with your partner.

Superb__ Good__ Fair__ Poor__ Very Poor__

Comments_____

2~ What attracted you the most to your partner?

(Choose 3) Sex__ Physical__ Intelligent__ Communicates well__
Personality__ Financial__ Influence of family/friends__
Similar backgrounds/interests__
Other_____

3~ If choosing a partner now, what would attract you the most?

(Choose 3) Sex__ Physical__ Intelligent__ Financial__
Communicates well__ Personality__ Influence of family/friends__
Similar backgrounds/interests__
Other_____

4~ Describe positive feelings you have with this partner.

(Choose as many as you want) Contented__ Loved__ Appreciated__
Satisfied__ Able to share feelings__ Equals__ Self-confident__
Calm__ Proud__ Sexually compatible__ Independent__
Other_____

5- Describe negative feeling you have with this partner. (Choose as many as you want)

Unloved__ Tied down__ Isolated__ Overwhelmed__ Trapped__
Unappreciated__ Afraid__ Dissatisfied__ Feel controlled__
Nervous__ Depressed__ Sexually frustrated__
Lonely__ Unable to share feelings__ None__
Other_____

6- How do you divide responsibilities between you two?
I have all__ I have the most__ Divided fairly__
Partner has the most__ Partner has all__

7- Conflicts with this partner. (Choose as many as you want)
Personal habits__ Infidelity__ Being ignored__ Financial__
Sex together__ Communication__ Children__ Family__ My job__
Partner's job__ Religion__ Politics__ Personal interests__
Alcohol/Drugs__ Other_____

8- How do you deal with stress? (Choose as many as you want)
Pray__ Meditate__ Yoga__ Exercise__ Cry__ Talk with partner__
Talk with friend__ Alcohol__ Drugs__ Tranquilizers__ Watch TV__
Social Media__ Express aggression__ Hobbies__
Other_____

9- In the past few months have you often had? Anger__
Depression__ Headaches__ Insomnia__ Irritability__ Anxiety__
Uninterested in sex__ Cry easily__ Stomach issues__
Feeling I can't go on__ Lonely__ Gaining or losing weight__
Tiring easily__ Guilty feeling__ Unable to concentrate__ Tense__
Worried__ Other_____

10~ What big change could your partner make to have this relationship work better? _____

11~ What big changes could you make to have this relationship work better? _____

12~Please rate your life overall.

Splendid ___ Good ___ Fair___ Poor___ Very Poor___

Comments_____

Any additional comments?

Date_____   CHANGE 1 BEHAVIOR; IMPROVE YOUR LIFE
Sharon W. Penn 2017   Email me: *sharonwpenn@gmail.com*

WORKSHEET 9

HEALTHY HABITS CHECKLIST

Please read Chapter 9: Focus On Healthy Living.

Please respond to the thirty questions using the following scale:

Never=1 **Rarely=2** **Sometimes=3**
Often=4 **Most of the time=5**

I get a physical checkup annually and see my health care provider as needed. ____

I exercise at least 10 minutes or more several times a week. ____

I eat a well-balanced diet at least five days a week. ____

I weigh close to my ideal weight. ____

I avoid alcoholic beverages. ____

I wear a seat belt in the car. ____

I avoid cigarettes, e-cigarettes, cigars, pipe, or vaping. ____

I only take prescribed or over-the-counter drugs. ____

I average sleeping at least 7 hours nightly. ____

I am happy and content. ____

I seldom worry about things I cannot change. ____

I face up to problems and cope with change. ____

I think positive thoughts. ____

Never=1   **Rarely=2**   **Sometimes=3**
　　Often=4   **Most of the time=5**

I read books and journals. ____

I do puzzles/games to keep my brain active. ____

I have an optimistic outlook on life. ____

I have a friend I can talk to about my life. ____

I am close with family and friends. ____

I have social or educational activities. ____

I easily express healthy emotions. ____

I respond to other people's feelings. ____

I am comfortable with other people. ____

I accept opinions of others. ____

I stick up for myself when necessary. ____

I pray or meditate. ____

I participate in spiritual rituals with others. ____

I know and accept my limitations. ____

I make decisions about my life. ____

I offer my time and assets to help others. ____

I forgive myself and others. ____

TOTAL YOUR SCORE _____

SCORING: Your responses on the Healthy Habit Checklist rate how well you take care of your health.

120 and above--Excellent: You're doing a great job of taking care of your health.

85 - 119--Average: You can do better to have good health.

84 and below--Poor: Bad habits may diminish your health.

Look at area on the test where you scored Never or Rarely, and begin to change one behavior at a time, starting today.

Date_____

Sharon W. Penn 2017

CHANGE 1 BEHAVIOR; IMPROVE YOUR LIFE

Email me: *sharonwpenn@gmail.com*

WORKSHEET 10

FRIENDSHIP CHECKLIST

Please read Chapter 10—Treasure Your Friendships.
This worksheet is used for both Chapters 4 and 10.

7 Tasks   Times Tried **2-10 X daily**

1-Smile Appropriately ---

2-Make Eye Contact ---

3-Greet/Get Response ---

4-Touch Appropriately ---

5-Use Open Body Language ---

6-Compliment Others ---

7-Say Name in Conversation ---

Please email me to tell me about your experiences.

Date_____   CHANGE 1 BEHAVIOR; IMPROVE YOUR LIFE
Sharon W. Penn 2017   *Email me: sharonwpenn@gmail.com*

WORKSHEET 11

AGE GRACEFULLY REVIEW

Please read Chapter 11-*Choose to Age Gracefully.*

Use the scale below to answer the 16 questions, based on the past month.

N=**Never**	*R=Rarely*	*S=Sometimes*
O=Often		*M=Most of the time*

1~ Do you present a positive attitude of yourself to others? _____

2~ Do you write your thoughts in a journal? If so, do you make a list of things and people that you are grateful for, and keep it current? _____

3~ Do you begin and/or end your day with a minute of deep breathing, and focus awareness of your body, thoughts, and feelings? _____

4~ Do you pray or meditate, and experience the activity with attentiveness? _____

5~ Do you spend quality time by hanging out with people you love or admire? _____

6~ If someone you love or admire lives far away, do you call, text, or email them? _____

7~ Do you do something to energize your body, e.g., stretching, walking, swimming, shaking your body to your favorite dance music, or some other fun physical activity? _____

8~ Do you focus on your health by proper eating, getting enough sleep, and drinking lots of filtered water? _____

9~ Do you try new things, e.g., a new hobby, a new skill, or make an effort to meet new people, or other new things? _____

10~ Do you regularly declutter your living or workspace? _____

11~ Do you keep your brain active by doing puzzles, crosswords, reading, etc? _____

12~ Do you avoid excessive sun exposure and use sunscreen daily? _____

13~Do you dress to suit your age? _____

14~ Do you avoid too much stress in your life? _____

15~ When you do have ongoing stress, do you practice calming yourself with prayer, meditation, yoga, exercise, walk outside, talk with someone, etc? _____

16~ If you don't have someone to take care of, do you have a pet or pets? _____

Total: Never ____ Rarely ____ Sometimes ____
Often ____ Most of the time ____

If you put *Often* or *Most of the time* on 7 or more questions, you may be aging gracefully.

If fewer than that, look at the questions you reported *Never, Rarely, or Sometimes;* and decide right now to do one of these at a time and make it a habit by doing it *Often* or *Most of the time.*

Date_____   CHANGE 1 BEHAVIOR; IMPROVE YOUR LIFE
Sharon W. Penn 2017   *Email me: sharonwpenn@gmail.com*

WORKSHEET 12

ARE YOU SPIRITUAL?

Please read Chapter 12: Seek Your Spirituality.

For a spirituality rating, please use this scale to respond:

Never=1   **Rarely=2**   **Sometimes=3**
Often=4   **Most of the time=5**

I feel connected to the spiritual aspects of life. ____

I am interested in things in life that cannot be scientifically explained. ____

I offer my time and possessions to help others. ____

I help protect people, animals, and plants. ____

I feel connected to nature. ____

I pray, do yoga, or meditate. ____

I participate in a church, or a spiritual or religious community or group. ____

I feel a sense of unity with things around me. ____

I trust my feelings more than my logical reasons. ____

I feel a spiritual connection with people. ____

I believe that miracles happen. ____

I have experiences that make my role in life clear. ____

I want to make the world a better place, like trying to prevent injustices. ____

SCORE-add your numbers _____

40-50 = You are spiritually aware.

30-39 = You are as spiritually aware as many other people.

11-29 = You can learn more about spiritual life.

10 and under = You resist spiritual awareness.

Date_____   CHANGE 1 BEHAVIOR; IMPROVE YOUR LIFE
Sharon W. Penn 2017   Email me: *sharonwpenn@gmail.com*

Chapter 13—Find Your Humor and Fun—has online exercises for you to try if you wish.

Use a search engine to find up-to-date quizzes. Type in *sense of humor quiz* to search.

So, I'll put the CHECKLIST and CONTRACT sheet, which is used for Chapters 4-14, the Behavior Chapters, as Worksheet 13. Please see on the next page.

WORKSHEET 13

To be completed and used in each chapter 4-14

CHECKLIST & CONTRACT

**I WILL COMPLETE THIS CHECKLIST & CONTRACT
FOR EACH BEHAVIOR I WORK ON.**

____ I am motivated to change/improve my behavior.
Name behavior:

____ I will begin by working to improve one behavior at a time.

____ I will complete this checklist for each behavior.

____ I will sign a contract and place it where I can see it often.

____ I will work with another person to improve this behavior.

____ I will keep a journal about my progress and feelings.

____ I will read Chapters 1 & 2.

____ I will complete the worksheets for Chapters 1 & 2.

____ I will read the chapter of the behavior I want to improve.

____ I will complete the worksheet(s) relevant to this chapter.

CONTRACT

As of today, I choose to improve my life, one behavior at a time, by:
behavior written here…

Name_____   Date_____

Date_____
Sharon W. Penn 2017

CHANGE 1 BEHAVIOR; IMPROVE YOUR LIFE
Email me: sharonwpenn@gmail.com

Print and Post

WORKSHEET 14

HABITS OF HAPPY PEOPLE

Please read Chapter 14-Help Yourself to Happiness.

Use the scale below to answer the 12
questions, based on the past month.

N=Never   *R=Rarely*   *S=Sometimes*
    O=Often   *M=Most of the time*

1-Do you have feelings of gratitude towards people and events from
your past and present? _____

2-Do you feel your life has purpose? _____

3-Are you optimistic about the future? _____

4-Are you able to focus on the present moment and not get distracted
by thoughts of the past or future? _____

5-Do you share feelings with friends or relatives? _____

6-Do you practice at least 5-20 min. of daily physical
exercise? _____

7-Do you have a pet or pets to take care of? _____

8-Do you offer to help out a friend, neighbor, or co-worker (babysit,
cook a meal, drive them someplace, accompany them as support,
etc.)? _____

9-Do you tell people you are grateful for what they do for you, or what
they have done for you in the past? _____

10~Do you engage in activities that you find challenging and absorbing (sports, writing, taking classes, attending a book club or other type club, etc.)? _____

11~Do you participate in a church, spiritual community or group? _____

12~Do you volunteer with a group that asks for help (hospital, school, nursing home, homeless shelter, animal shelter, etc.)? _____

Scoring:

If you put *Often* or *Most of the time* on 5 or more questions, you may be satisfied with your life.

If fewer than that, begin to look at the questions you reported *Never* or *Rarely,* and decide now to do one of these at a time: *Often* or *Most of the time.*

Notice numbers 5-12 are action questions. If you do these first, you may see numbers 1-4 change to: *Often.*

Date_____   CHANGE 1 BEHAVIOR; IMPROVE YOUR LIFE
Sharon W. Penn 2017   *Email me: sharonwpenn@gmail.com*

POSTERS FOR BEHAVIOR CHANGES

Penn's DOs and DON'Ts
Posters on the following pages are in alphabetical order.

AGING GRACEFULLY

ANGER CONTROL

APPROACHABILITY

ARGUE MATURELY

BLUES BUSTERS

FRIENDSHIP

HABIT CHANGE

HAPPINESS

HEALTHY LIVING

MENTAL WELL-BEING

RELATIONSHIPS

SELF-ESTEEM

SPIRITUALITY

AGING GRACEFULLY – Penn's DOs and DON'Ts

~DO CHOOSE A POSITIVE ATTITUDE.

~DO HAVE FUN.

~DO FOCUS ON YOUR HEALTH.

~DO PRESERVE YOUR MEMORY.

~DO MANAGE YOUR PAIN.

~DO RELAXATION TECHNIQUES.

~DO KEEP SAFETY IN MIND.

~DO BE SOCIAL.

~DO SEEK YOUR SPIRITUALITY.

~DON'T OVEREAT.

~DON'T SMOKE.

~DON'T ALLOW STRESS.

~DON'T ABUSE ALCOHOL OR DRUGS.

Print and post where you and others will see it.
For more details, please see Chapter 11 of *Change 1 Behavior, Improve Your Life.* 2017
Sharon W. Penn   *Email me: sharonwpenn@gmail.com*

Sharon W. Penn

ANGER CONTROL – Penn's DOs and DON'Ts

~DO decide if you are going to let other people control your behavior.

~DO know you choose to show anger.

~DO know you choose to turn away.

~DO know you choose to relax.

~DO talk it out when the anger is gone.

~DO avoid criticizing.

~DO use humor.

~DO know you can apologize.

~DO say, "I won by staying calm."

~DON'T count to ten; use a positive statement instead.

~DON'T FORGET- only one thing at a time. Pick one and do it now.

Print and post where you and others will see it.
For more details, please see Chapter 7 of *Change 1 Behavior, Improve Your Life.* 2017
Sharon W. Penn   *Email me: sharonwpenn@gmail.com*

APPROACHABILITY- Penn's DOs and DON'Ts

DAILY:

~DO SMILE Appropriately at 2-10 People.

~DO MAKE EYE CONTACT with 2-10 People.

~DO GREET 2-10 People.

~DO TOUCH Appropriately 2-10 People.

~DO SHOW Open Body Language.

~DO Compliment 2-10 People.

~DO Say Their Name in Conversation to 2-10 people.

~DO ONE BEHAVIOR AT A TIME until they all become habits.

~DON'T STOP until they all become habits. Soon, you will have mastered all of them.

Print and post where you and others will see it.

For more details, please see Chapters 4 and 10 of *Change 1 Behavior; Improve Your Life.* 2017
Sharon W. Penn   *Email me: sharonwpenn@gmail.com*

ARGUE MATURELY- Penn's DOs and DON'Ts

~DO LISTEN. See the other point of view.

~DO ASK FOR TIME to think about what's being said.

~DO KNOW WOMEN and MEN DEAL with CONFLICT DIFFERENTLY.

~DO FIND a "WIN-WIN" SOLUTION.

~DO KNOW FORGIVENESS HAS TO TAKE PLACE for the process to be complete.

~DON'T GET SIDE-TRACKED. Take one issue at a time, and keep to the point.

~DON'T TALK ABOUT TOO MANY THINGS AT ONCE.

~DON'T FORGET- only one thing at a time.

~DO PICK ONE AND DO IT NOW!

Print and post where you and others will see it.

For more details, please see Chapter 8 of *Change 1 Behavior; Improve Your Life.* 2017
Sharon W. Penn   *Email me: sharonwpenn@gmail.com*

BLUES BUSTERS – Penn's DOs and DON'Ts

~DO YOGA, TAKE A WALK, or EXERCISE.

~DO SCHEDULE SOCIAL EVENTS.

~DO HAVE LOVING RELATIONSHIPS.

~DO CREATE SUCCESS FOR YOURSELF.

~DO HELP SOMEONE IN NEED.

~DO TREAT YOURSELF to PLEASURE.

~DO EXPRESS APPRECIATION.

~DO WRITE in a GRATITUDE JOURNAL.

~DO PRAY and MEDITATE.

~DON'T FORGET- TAKE ONE STEP at a TIME.

Print and post where you and others will see it.

For more details, please see Chapter 6 of *Change 1 Behavior, Improve Your Life.* 2017
Sharon W. Penn   *Email me: sharonwpenn@gmail.com*

FRIENDSHIP – Penn's DOs and DON'Ts

~DO PLAN ACTIVITIES WITH FRIENDS.

~DO GIVE UNCONDITIONAL SUPPORT.

~DO GIVE ACCEPTANCE, LOYALTY, and TRUST.

~DO SHARE YOUR LIFE WITH FRIENDS.

~DO LISTEN TO THEM.

~DO INTERACT- WRITE, CALL, or VISIT.

~DO CONFIDE THOUGHTS, NEEDS, FEELINGS, and FEARS.

~DO ASK FOR WHAT YOU WANT.

~DO ADD NEW FRIENDS TO YOUR CIRCLE; ASSESS THEM FIRST.

~DON'T CRITICIZE FRIENDS.

~DON'T DO ALL THE GIVING.

~DON'T EVER BETRAY A CONFIDENCE.

Print and post where you and others will see it.

For more details, please see Chapter 10 of *Change 1 Behavior, Improve Your Life.* 2017
Sharon W. Penn   *Email me: sharonwpenn@gmail.com*

HABIT CHANGE – Penn's DOs and DON'Ts

~DO DEFINE EACH GOAL and MAKE IT MEASURABLE.

~DO DIVIDE the TASKS into SUB-GOALS.

~DO AFFIRMATIONS & VISUALIZATIONS.

~DO WRITE the NEW HABIT ON a CARD.

~DO DEVISE a REPLACEMENT ACTION.

~DO USE HABIT MONITORS.

~DO ASK FOR HELP.

~DON'T DEMAND PERFECTION.

~DON'T FORGET - ONLY ONE AT A TIME.

~DO BEGIN NOW!

Print and post where you and others will see it.

For more details, please see Chapter 2 of *Change 1 Behavior, Improve Your Life.* 2017
Sharon W. Penn   *Email me: sharonwpenn@gmail.com*

HAPPINESS - Penn's DOs and DON'Ts

~DO SMILE OFTEN.

~DO THINK and EXPRESS GRATITUDE.

~DO GOOD DEEDS.

~DO STAY CLOSE with FAMILY and FRIENDS.

~DO NOTICE HOW OTHER HAPPY PEOPLE ACT.

~DON'T ALLOW NEGATIVITY TO RULE YOUR LIFE.

~DON'T DWELL ON THE PAST.

~DON'T LIVE WITH REGRETS.

~DON'T PUT YOURSELF DOWN.

~DON'T FORGET- only one at a time.

Print and post where you and others will see it.

For more details, please see Chapter 14 of *Change 1 Behavior; Improve Your Life.* 2017
Sharon W. Penn   *Email me: sharonwpenn@gmail.com*

HEALTHY LIVING - Diet, Exercise, Sleep
Penn's DOs and DON'Ts

~DO EAT MORE VEGETABLES, FRUITS, NUTS; FEWER REFINED GRAINS, AND FEWER SUGARS.

~DO CUT PORTION SIZES, IF DIETING.

~DO HAVE A SUPPORT SYSTEM IF DIETING AND EXERCISING.

~DO KEEP A REGULAR SCHEDULE FOR EXERCISING.

~DO AVOID STRESS.

~DO GET PLENTY OF SLEEP.

~DO FOLLOW TIPS FOR INSOMNIACS.

~DO USE SLEEP AIDS.

~DON'T TAKE DAY NAPS IF YOU'RE AN INSOMNIAC.

~DON'T READ AN EXCITING BOOK JUST BEFORE SLEEPTIME.

Print and post where you and others will see it.

For more details, please see Chapter 9 of *Change 1 Behavior; Improve Your Life.* 2017
Sharon W. Penn   *Email me: sharonwpenn@gmail.com*

MENTAL WELL-BEING
Penn's DOs and DON'Ts

~DO HAVE A PURPOSE FOR YOUR LIFE.

~DO HAVE A POSITIVE ATTITUDE.

~DO HAVE GOOD RELATIONSHIPS.

~DO CONTINUE PERSONAL GROWTH.

~DO CONTROL YOUR LIFE.

~DO KEEP FAMILY AND FRIENDS CLOSE.

~DO COPE WITH ADVERSITY.

~DO HAVE A SPIRITUAL LIFE.

~DO PHYSICAL ACTIVITIES.

~DO RELAXATION EXERCISES.

~DO MANAGE STRESS.

~DON'T NEGLECT YOUR HEALTH.

~DON'T FORGET- only one thing at a time.

Print and post where you and others will see it.

For more details, please see Chapter 1 of *Change 1 Behavior; Improve Your Life.* 2017
Sharon W. Penn   *Email me: sharonwpenn@gmail.com*

RELATIONSHIPS – Penn's DOs and DON'Ts

~**DO CHERISH and NOURISH THE IMPORTANT PEOPLE IN YOUR LIFE.**

~**DO COMPLIMENT WITH SPECIFICS.**

~**DO NOTICE THEM OFTEN.**

~**DO TELL THEM OFTEN HOW IMPORTANT THEY ARE TO YOU.**

~**DO HAVE *SIT-DOWN* REVIEWS TOGETHER.**

~**DON'T TURN AWAY.**

~**DON'T FORGET- ONLY ONE THING AT A TIME.**

~**DO PICK ONE AND DO IT NOW!**

Print and post where you and others will see it.

For more details, please see Chapter 8 of *Change 1 Behavior; Improve Your Life.* 2017
Sharon W. Penn   *Email me: sharonwpenn@gmail.com*

SELF-ESTEEM - Penn's DOs & DON'Ts

~DO SOMETHING EVERY DAY YOU DO WELL.

~DO LEARN SOMETHING NEW EVERY DAY.

~DO WHAT MAKES YOU FEEL GOOD.

~DO ASSOCIATE WITH PEOPLE YOU ADMIRE.

~DO BE HONEST WITH OTHERS.

~DO HELP NEEDY PEOPLE.

~DON'T TELL LIES or HALF-TRUTHS.

~DON'T SMOKE, OVEREAT, or ABUSE ALCOHOL or DRUGS.

~DON'T BE VICTIMIZED BY OTHERS.

~DON'T NEGLECT YOUR HEALTH.

~DON'T FORGET- only one thing at a time.

Print and post where you and others will see it.

For more details, please see Chapter 5 of *Change 1 Behavior; Improve Your Life.* 2017
Sharon W. Penn   *Email me: sharonwpenn@gmail.com*

SPIRITUALITY – Penn's DOs and DON'Ts

~DO KNOW YOU ARE A SPIRITUAL BEING HAVING A HUMAN EXPERIENCE.

~DO KEEP YOUR LIFE'S PURPOSE IN MIND WHEN DECISION MAKING.

~DO CONNECT TO THE SPIRITUAL ASPECTS OF LIFE.

~DO OFFER YOUR TIME and POSSESSIONS TO HELP PROTECT PEOPLE, ANIMALS, and PLANTS.

~DO STAY CLOSELY CONNECTED TO FAMILY and FRIENDS.

~DO PARTICIPATE IN A CHURCH, OR A SPIRITUAL OR RELIGIOUS COMMUNITY OR GROUP.

~DO YOGA, PRAY, or MEDITATE DAILY.

~DO TRUST YOUR FEELINGS MORE THAN LOGICAL REASONING.

~DON'T FORGET- ONLY ONE BEHAVIOR AT A TIME WHEN MAKING A CHANGE.

Print and post where you and others will see it.

For more details, please see Chapter 12-*Change 1 Behavior; Improve Your Life.* 2017
Sharon W. Penn   *Email me: sharonwpenn@gmail.com*

Chapter Notes

Notes for the Introduction

To exist is to change: "Henri Bergson quotes—Thinkexist.com." *http://thinkexist. com/quotation/to exist />.* Web. 29 Jul 2016

Change occurs through relearning: *Quote of Margaret Click, Ph.D., Change1Behavior* Research Gp. Consultant. 2004

Never doubt that a small group: "Margaret Mead-Wikiquote." *http://en.wikiquote.org/wiki/Margaret Mead>.* Web. 29 Jul 2016

The joy of life is living it: "Improvement-Edgar Albert Guest-PoemHunter.com." *http://www.poemhunter.com/best-poems/edgar-albert-guest/improvement-4/* Web 13 Aug. 2016

Notes for Chapter 1-Mentally Healthy People

As a single footstep will not make a path on the earth: "The Henry D. Thoreau Quotation Page/ Walden Woods." *<http://www.walden.org/Library/Quotations/ Quotation Page>. Web.14 Jul 2016*

Counselors at The Center in Orlando can also provide vouchers for free ongoing therapy, or you can print out a voucher at*<http://twospiritshealth.org/pulse-voucher-program>. The Orlando Sentinel. July 30, 2016*

Rate Your Mental Well-Being: Many of the items used in the design of Worksheet 1 were taken from an article by Richard H. Price, Ph. D., Professor of Psychology at the University of Michigan. Feb. 2004

University of Central Florida (UCF) in Orlando, has a program called **RESTORES** (Center for **RES**earch and **T**reatment **o**n **R**esponse to **E**xtreme **S**tressors). They specialize in anxiety and PTSD. Call: 407-823-3910. *Ibid.*

MENTAL HEALTH RESOURCES -- *rtor.org* is a gateway website that helps families find resources and support for loved ones with mental health concerns. For help with treatments and services or to obtain a referral to an RtoR Family-Endorsed mental health provider call their Resource Line to speak with a Resource Specialist. **Phone: (203) 724-9070.**

The Resource Specialists can answer your questions about mental health services and RtoR Family-Endorsed Providers featured on this site. If a representative is not available to answer your call, please leave a message, and they will respond at the earliest opportunity. Please note: **This is not a crisis line. If you need immediate help, call 911, or contact your local crisis services.**

Mental Health.gov provides one-stop access to U.S. government mental health information. Mental health resources are now available in Spanish.

The National Suicide Prevention Lifeline – If you or someone you know needs help, call 1-800-TALK (8255) immediately. This 24-hour service is available to anyone in need of help. Never ignore or underestimate remarks about suicide. If you think your friend or relative is in immediate danger, do not leave him or her alone – stay there and call 911 or the **National Suicide Prevention Lifeline at 1-800-273-TALK (8255).**

United States Department of Veterans Affairs
www.mentalhealth.va.gov

Veterans Crisis Line Mental Health Awareness Provider Toolkit. Authoritative mental health information and resources for Veterans and their families.
www.parentcenterhub.org/repository/mental health

PLEASE NOTE: Crisis Intervention Training (CIT) – with a 40-hour curriculum – is the most comprehensive police officer mental health training program in the country. According to Laura Usher, CIT program manager at NAMI headquarters in Arlington, Virginia, there are crisis intervention training programs in states as well as the District of Columbia. (check to see if your state has CIT.) How Police Officers Are (or Aren't) Trained... *http://www.theatlantic.com/health/2013* Web. 20 Nov. 2016

Notes for Chapter 2- Change a Habit

A habit is defined as an involuntary pattern: "Bad Habits-Swati Salunkhe" *http://Swatisalunkhe.com/bad-habit* Web. 27 Sep 2016

To change your behavior or habit: *Ibid*

As a single footstep will not make a path on the earth: "The Henry D. Thoreau Mis-Quotation Page/ Walden Woods." *<http://www.walden.org/Library/Quotations/ Quotation Page>. Web.14 Jul 2016*

Whatever you can do, or dream you can do,: "GSNA? Quotes: Commitment." *<http://www.goethesociety.org/pages/quotecom/ Web.14 Jul 2016*

Notes for Chapter 3- Addiction

We may think there is willpower involved... George A. Sheehan. *http://www. brainyquote.com/quotes/george a sheehan.html* 16 Nov. 2016

Babor, T.F., et al., *AUDIT: The Alcohol Use Disorders Identification Test. Guidelines for Use in Primary Care. World Health Organization, Department of Mental Health and Substance Dependence.* *<http://whqlibdoc.who.int/2001/WHO MSD MSB 01.6a.pdf. WHO.>* Web. 14 Jul 2016

Notes for Chapter 4- Approachability

Salespeople receive training on how to greet customers: *http://www.trainingcoursematerial.com>* Web. *14 Jul 2016*

For human beings, you need two hugs a day to survive: *<www.brainyquote.com/ quotes/quotes/v/virginiasa175185.html>* Web. 14 Jul 2016

Notes for Chapter 5-Self-Esteem

Never forget that you are one of a kind: *TOP 25 QUOTES BY R. BUCKMINSTER FULLER (of 341) | A-Z* Quotes. *<http://www.azquotes.com/ author/5231-R Buckminster Fuller>* Web. 23 Jul 2016.

Your answers to these types of questions may vary from day-to-day: Article on Self-Esteem by Margaret Click, Ph.D. unpublished. Permission to quote. 2003

Notes for Chapter 6-Blues Busters

If you always do what you've always done…:, Researchers have only been able to trace the quote back to the 1980s. The earliest instance located by quote investigator appeared in "The Milwaukee Sentinel" of Milwaukee, Wisconsin in 1981. The speaker was an educator and counselor on family relationships and human sexuality named Jessie Potter who worked for a non-profit organization she founded. *<http:// www.quoteinvestigator.com/2016/04/25/get/>* Web. 23 Jul 2016

Stanford Medicine says scientists look at patterns of illness: Major Depression and Genetics.
<http://depressiongenetics.stanford.edu/mddandgenes.html>
Web. 20 Sept 2016

Information for the Depression Scale is taken from material in DSM-5: American Psychiatric Association. The newest edition of Diagnostic and Statistical Manual of Mental Disorders (*DSM-5*®) is the product of more than 10 years of effort by hundreds of international experts in all aspects of mental health. Their dedication and hard work have yielded an authoritative volume that defines and classifies mental disorders in order to improve diagnoses, treatment, and research. *<https://www. psychiatry.org/psychiatrists/>* Web. 23 Jul 2016

Notes for Chapter 7-Anger

Once, after he had attacked her, she asked why: "Ex-Wife Says Orlando Shooter Might Have Been Hiding…" *<http://www.yahoo.com/news/ex-wife-says-orlando-shooter-105927115>. Web.15 July 2016*

Violence is not inevitable, it is learned. And it can be unlearned,: Esta Soler, a founder of Futures Without Violence @TED Talks. <*http.www.futureswithoutviolence. org*> Web. 15 Jul 2016

Try this breathing exercise: Ask the expert: Prevention. Dec. 2016

Notes for Chapter 8-Relationships

PARENT-CHILD RELATIONSHIPS: A Bibliography

Bailey, Rebecca Anne. I love you rituals *1st ed.* 2000 *I Love You Rituals offers more than seventy delightful rhymes and games that send the message of unconditional love and enhance children's social, emotional, and school success. Winner of a 1999 Parent's Guide Children's Media Award.*

Berman, Jenn. The A to Z guide to raising happy, confident kids 2007 *Parents no longer have time to read long books about the theories of parenting. What they want are quick pieces of advice geared to their busy lifestyles and immediate needs. Dr. Jenn comes to the rescue.*

Blau, Melinda. Family Whispering: the baby whisperer's commonsense strategies for communicating and connecting with the people you love. 2014 *The long awaited Baby Whisperer's guide to building a strong and loving family.*

Chapman, Gary D. Growing up social: raising relational kids in a screen-driven world. 2014 *Is technology bringing your family closer together or driving you farther apart? In this digital age, children are spending more and more time interacting with a screen and less time playing outside, reading a book, or interacting.*

DeSteno, David. The truth about trust [electronic resource]: how it determines success in life, love, learning, and more. 2014 *What really drives success and failure? Can I trust you? It's the question that strikes at the heart of human existence, whether we're talking about business partnerships, romantic relationships, or child-parent bonds.*

Garrison, Brenda. Love no matter what: when your kids make decisions you don't agree with. 2013 *Parents and kids will never agree on everything but what can mom and dad do when that decision--whether a matter of preference, spirituality, or morality.*

Hall, Philip S. Parenting a defiant child: a sanity-saving guide to finally stopping the bad behavior. 2007 *Defiant children can be abrasive, irritating, and aggressive, intentionally provoking adults, defying authority, and antagonizing siblings.*

Karres, Erika V. Shearin. The everything parent's guide to raising girls: all you need to help your daughter develop confidence, achieve self-esteem, and improve communication *2nd ed.* 2014

Meeker, Margaret J. Boys should be boys: 7 secrets to raising healthy sons. 2003

Strauch, Barbara. The primal teen: what the new discoveries about the teenage brain tell us about our kids *1st ed.* 2003

these intimacy bonds reflect deep primal survival needs: *Dr. Susan Johnson, Are You There for Me? The Psychotherapy Networker. <https://www.psychotherapynetworker. org/ blog/details/402/are-you-there-for-me>* Web. 19 Sept 2014

Dr. John Gottman has been studying couples for more than 20 years*: The Relationship Cure. 2001.* John Gottman, Ph.D. & Joan LeClaire.

Couples are invited to his "Love Lab," in Seattle, WA.: "John Gottman can assess your marriage in five minutes." *<http://www.automaticromantic.com/weblog/2008/ gottman-can-assess-your>*Web. 15 Jul 2016

Dr. Gottman gives the couples some privacy: *Ibid*

Couples argue; sometimes they argue a lot and sometimes a little: *Ibid*

Notes for Chapter 9- Healthy Living

Gaples Institute for Integrative Cardiology—a nonprofit that balances natural strategies with conventional medicine: *<http://www.gaplesinstitute.org.>* Web. 13 Jul 2016

They suggest that eating lots of vegetables and fruit leave less room for junk food: "Gaples' Institute Nutritional Facts." *<http://www.gaplesinstitute.org.>* Web. 13 Jul 2016

A study explains why people who eat nuts regularly have a significantly lower risk of heart disease: *Ibid*

Part of the explanation is that nuts are not completely digested: *Ibid*

WebMD says it's important to establish: Sleep Disorders: *http://webmd.com/ women/guide-tips.* Web. 17 Nov. 2016

When we hug or kiss someone we love: Step2Cortex sends info. *http://www. coursehero.com/file/p4bo3h9* Web. 17 Nov. 2016

Turn off your cell phone: How To Get Your Best Night's Sleep Ever. Prevention. *http://www.prevention.com* Web. 17 Nov. 2016

Light-emitting devices: *Ibid*

Some sleep experts say a late dinner: *http://webmd.com/women/guide-tips.* Web. 17 Nov. 2016

An alcoholic nightcap-tempting though it may be when you can't sleep: *http://www.backoutofwhack.com/wp/health-habits/10-simple-cures-for-insomnia/* Web. 18 Nov. 2016

Weight-loss pills: 12 Surprising Sources of Caffeine-*http://www.health.com* Web. 13 Jul. 2016

Many pain relievers incorporate caffeine to ease the pain: *Ibid*

Consider this simple, two ingredient solution for getting a great night's sleep: *Mix Two Ingredients Before Bed and Never Wake Up Tired Again. http://www.whydon'tyoutrythis.com.>* Web. 13 Jul 2016

This sea salt*: Ibid*

Herbal Teas - From hibiscus to mint to chamomile, the possibilities are practically endless when it comes to herbal teas: *Caffeine-free Hot Drinks. <http://www.thekitchen.com*
Web. 13 Jul 2016

I feel calm… I feel relaxed… I feel in control…: Author House. Franks, Dennis. *IN: Inhale and Relax. 2013*

Breathing Exercise: Relaxation Exercise for Falling Asleep: *http://www.meditationoasis.com/how-to-meditate/ simple-meditations/breathing-meditations* Web. 18 Nov. 2016

Guided Imagery: USC Center for Work and Family Life. *<http://www.cwfl.usc.edu/wellness/sleephandouts.*
Web. 10 Nov 2016

Notes for Chapter 10- Friendship

One of the most beautiful qualities of true friendship: <*http://www.brainyquotes. com*> Web. 17 Nov. 2016

Since intimacy is the keystone of friendship:
"*Six Ways to Make Friends*". Psychology Today.. <*http://www.psychologytoday.com.*> Web. 13 Jul 2016

Notes for Chapter 11- Age Gracefully

There is a fountain of youth: Sofia Loren. *http://www.brainyquotes.com* Web. 17 Nov. 2016

Everything can be taken from a man but one thing: Viktor Frankl (1959) *Man's Search for Meaning.*

The remarkable thing is, we have a choice every day: "*The Grace Awakening*" Swindoll, Charles. 1990 <*http://www.goodreads.com*> Web. 13 Jul 2016
We cannot change the fact: *Ibid*

looked at surveys taken by 386 men and women in 1968: Becca R. Levy, Ph.D. *Can attitudes toward aging affect how well we age?* <*www.bakadesayo.com/2009*> Web. 13 Jul 2016

In another study: *Ibid*

The discouraging one: *Ibid*

Five nonagenarians were asked to explain their longevity: *Attitudes Toward Aging Can Affect How Well We Age. WSJ www.wsj.com/2009* Web. 13 Jul 2016

Don't smoke: Smokers, I must warn you *http://answers.yahoo.com* Web. 17 Nov. 2016

Exercise increases capillary development in the brain: 7 Anti-Aging Tips. *http:// www.rd.com* Web. 17 Nov. 2016

Exercise helps protect and improve your brain function: (2015) "*Exercise Slows Brain Aging by 10 Years.*" Joseph Mercola, M.D. <*http://www.fitness.mercola.com Web.13 Jul 2016*

One study showed that strength training in the elderly: Weight Lifting and Brain Power? – *http://www.fitnessandphilosophy.org/blog/>* Web. 13 Jul 2016

I attended an excellent seminar in 2011: *"Protecting the Aging Brain: Focus on Nutrition and Mind/Body Health,"* Gary W. Arendash, Ph.D., research professor, University of South Florida, now President and CEO of NeuroEM Therapeutics, Inc., Phoenix, AZ. He gave permission to share his materials.

Moonwalking with Einstein: The Art and Science of Remembering Everything. Foer, Joshua, 2011.Penguin Press, N.Y.

Remember to put your car keys beside your bed at night: *http://www. crimestoppersatlantic.com/main/newsitems/ carkeys.asp>* Web. 15 Nov 2016

Meditation-Supposedly, meditators process pain differently than non-meditators. Web. 26 Sept 2016
https://www.psychologytoday.com /experts/kelly-mcgonigal-phd

Notes for Chapter 12-Spirituality

Just as a candle cannot burn without fire: "Just as a candle cannot burn without fire…Brainy Quote." *http://www.brainyquote.com/quotes/b/buddha121.* Web. 06 Aug 2016

Enlightened leadership is spiritual: *Deepak Chopra on Enlightened Leadership-* Forbes. *<http://www.forbes.com*
Web. 13 Jul 2016

Focused meditation is one type where you choose to focus on only one thing: *"Why People Who Pray Are Healthier Than Those Who Don't."* July 2016. <http://www. huffingtonpost.com *Web. 13 Jul 2016*

the relaxation response occurs when we pray: *Ibid*

At the University of Pennsylvania: "The Ethics of Neuroenhancement: Where Should the Line Be…"
http://journals/ww.com/neurotodayonline/. Web. 23 Aug 2016

Studies *at Bowling Green State University*: *"Why People Who Pray Are Healthier Than Those Who Don't."* July 2016. <http://www.huffingtonpost.com *Web. 13 Jul 2016*

Other studies: *Ibid*

The proper way to pray is to pour out our hearts to God: *"What Is the proper way to pray?" July 9, 2016. <http://www.gotquestions.org Web. 13 Jul 2016*

Also, pray by sitting, standing, or kneeling..."Prayer, the Great Adventure". Jeremiah, Dr. David. 2004.

Prayer is not merely a technique to heal illness and promote physical health: *"Why People Who Pray Are Healthier Than Those Who Don't." July 2016. http://www. huffingtonpost.com Web. 13 Jul 2016*

Notes for Chapter 13-Humor and Fun

Your sense of humor is one of the most powerful tools: "Laughter Is the Best Medicine: The Health Benefits of..." <http://*www.helpguide.org Web. 10 Jul 2016*

Laugh at yourself: *Ibid*

LAUGHTER AS MEDICINE: *"Spiritual Humor—Enlightened Spirituality". <www. enlightened-spirituality.org> Web.10 Jul 2016*

If you want a kitten: "Dribbleglass.com-Advice from kids." *<http://www.dribbleglass.com/jokes/advice.html.>* Web. 09 Nov 2016

If your dog doesn't like: 'Talented and Gifted Presentation by Dr. Jim Delisle." *<http://www.scps.K12.va.us./cirriculum/tag/workshophandouts.pdf>*. Web. 09 Nov 2016

Just keep banging on the door until someone opens: "Really Important Stuff Your Kids Can Teach You: *http://home.hiwaay.net/~thargrav/is.html>. Web.09 Nov 2016*

You shouldn't ask to start over: *Ibid*

Sherlock Holmes: One of Marilyn's Favorite Jokes-parade.com *<http://parade. com/514392/marilynvossavant/one-of-marilyns-favorite-jokes/ >* Web. 09 Nov 2016

A middle-aged woman: Jokes-Ricks Workshop Creations." *<http://www.rickswoodshopcreations.com/fun and >* Web. 09 Nov 2016

A little old man: *Ibid*

The main reason Santa is so jolly: *<www.brainyquote.com/quotes/quotes/g/georgecarl385341.html>* Web. 09 Nov 2016

What's the difference between: Question: What's the Difference Between A Snowman And A Snowwoman *<http://www.anvari.org/shortjoke/Quetions and Answers/whats-the-difference>*. Web. 09 Nov 2016

Lawyer: Doctor, do you recall: "Courtroom Testimony-AmigaMCCC." *<http://amigamccc.org/journal/0709cout.html>* Web. 09 Nov 2016

Lawyer: Doctor, before you performed: "Attorney Quotes-National Educational Seminars." *http://www.txseminars.com/index.php/attorney-quotes.* Web. 09 Nov 2016

A student was asked to list: "Religious Humor-Life Nets." *http://www.org/lighter/hum-rel.html.* Web. 09 Nov 2016

I was at the beach with my children: "What Happened To Him? careandkindness. org": *http://www.careandkindness.org/capsules/what happened* Web. 09 Nov 2016

No matter how hard you try: "Starfish-Changing Hearts Changes Lives." <http://*starfishcare.com/index.html>* Web. 09 Nov 2016

You can't trust dogs to watch your food: *Ibid*

Puppies still have bad breath: "Dribbleglass.com-Advice from kids." *http://www.dribbleglass.com/jokes/advice.html>.* Web. 09 Nov 2016

Helpguide.org gives us some more help: "Laughter Is the Best Medicine" *<http://www.helpguide.org Web. 10 Jul 2016*

There is a purifying power in laughter: "The Humor League-Timeline/Facebook." *http://www.facebook.com/ thehumorleague.photo>* Web. 09 Nov 2016

Notes for Chapter 14-Happiness

Sometimes your pet really can be your best friend: *"Depression Tips: Exercise, Diet, Stress…"* *<http://www.webmd.com> Web. 10 Jul 2016*

In our daily lives…happiness… <https://www.goodreads.com/author/quotes/4182. David_Steindl_Rast> Web. 25 Nov. 2016

Notes for Chapter 15-Quotes and Other Thoughts

Quotes found in the Introduction and Chapters 1-14 show the resources in Chapter Notes. The following resources are for the quotes not earlier identified:

ON THIS DAY…Mend a quarrel: Shannon, Maggie Oman, ed., Prayers for Healing: 365 Blessings, Poems, & Meditations from Around the World. Conari Press. 1999.

TEN POWER FOODS that Lower Blood Pressure: *www.prevention.com/food/13-power-foods-that-lower-blood-pressure-naturally>* Web. 15 Apr 2014

Forget the chest-clutching you've seen in the movies: *http://parade.com/417280/…/heart-attacks-testing-yourself-and-knowing-risks/* Web. 21 Aug 2015

Key Numbers for Heart Health: Cholesterol, Blood Pressure, Waist Size *www.webmd.com/heart/features/do-you-know-your-heart-numbers* > Web. 12 Nov 2016

5 WAYS TO PROTECT YOUR HEART EVERY DAY: *http://parade.com/417222/…/5-ways-to-protect-your-heart-every-day/* Web. 21 August 2015

STROKE WARNING SIGNS / THINK F.A.S.T.: *http://www.strokeassociation.org/STROKEORG/WarningSigns>* Web. 12 Nov 2016

A Bibliography

More to Explore

for

CHANGE 1 BEHAVIOR, IMPROVE YOUR LIFE

Amen, D. *Change Your Brain, Change Your Life.*
N.Y. Three Rivers Press. 1998

Amen, D. *Magnificent Mind....*
N.Y. Three Rivers Press. 2008

Beck, A., *Love is Never Enough: Relationship Problems.* N.Y. HarperPerennial.1988

Borysenko, J. *Minding the Body, Mending the Mind.*
N.Y. Bantam Books.1987

Brantley, J. *Calming Your Anxious Mind.*
Oakland, CA. New Harbinger Pub. Inc.2003

Burns, D. *Feeling Good Handbook.*
N.Y. Plume Book.1989

Burns, D. *Feeling Good Together.*
N.Y. Broadway Books. 2008

Campbell, S. *Couple's Journey: Intimacy...*
San Luis, CA. Impact Publishers. 1980

Casey, K. *Change Your Mind & Your Life Will Follow.*
Boston, MA. Conari Press. 2005

Childre, D. *Transforming Stress...*
Oakland, CA. New Harbinger Pub. Inc. 2005

Clifton, D. *Soar with Your Strengths.*
N.Y., Dell Trade Paperback.1992

Copeland, M. *Depression Workbook.*
Oakland, CA. New Harbinger, Pub. Inc. 2001

Covey, S. *7 Habits of Highly Effective People.*
N.Y. Simon & Schuster. 1989

Davison, T. *Trust the Force*:
N.J. Jason Aronson, Inc.1995

DiGiuseppe, R. *Understanding Anger Disorders.*
N.Y. Oxford Univ. Press. 2007

Doka, K. *Living with Grief: When Illness is Prolonged.*
Bristol, PA. Taylor & Francis Pub.1997

Dyer, W. *Power of Intention.*
Carlsbad, CA. Hay House, Inc.2004

Enright, R. *Helping Clients Forgive.*
Washington, D.C. Amer. Psychological Assoc. 2000

Foer, Joshua. *Moonwalking with Einstein: The Art and Science of Remembering Everything.,*
N.Y. The Penguin Press, 2011

Glick, I. Ed. Treating Depression.
San Francisco. Jossey-Bass Pub.1995

Gold, M., Good News about Depression.
N.Y. Bantam Books.1995

Goleman, D. Emotional Intelligence.
N.Y. Bantam Books.1995

Gottman, J. 7 Principles for Making Marriage Work.
N.Y. Three Rivers Press.1999

Gottman, J. Relationship Cure: 5 Step Guide…
N.Y. Three Rivers Press. 2001

Gray, J. Men Are from Mars, Women Are from Venus.
N.Y. HarperPerennial.1992

Greenberger, D. Mind over Mood: Change How You Feel. N.Y. Guilford Pres. 1995

Groopman, J. Anatomy of Hope.
N.Y. Random House.2004

Hart, L. Winning family: Increasing Self-Esteem.
Berkeley, CA. Celestial Arts.1993

Hayes, J. Smart Love.
LA, CA. Jeremy Tarcher, Inc.1989

Karasu, T. Psychotherapy for Depression.
N.J. Jason Aronson, Inc.1990

Kassinove, H. ed. Anger Disorders.
Wash. D.C. Taylor & Francis.1995

Klass, D. ed. Continuing Bonds...Grief.
Wash. D.C. Taylor & Francis. 1996

Klein, A. Healing Power of Humor.
N.Y. Jeremy Tarcher/Putnam. 1989

Klein, D. Understanding Depression...
N.Y. Oxford University Press.1993

Larson, J. Depression-Free...7 Weeks to Eliminate
Anxiety. N.Y. Ballantine Publishing.1999

Lazarus, P. Healing the Mind the Natural Way.
N.Y. G.P.Putnum's Sons. 1995

Lorayne, H. Ageless Memory.
N.Y. Black Dog & Leventhal Pub. 2007

Luskin, F. Forgive for Good.
N.Y.HarperCollins Pub. 2002

McKay, M. When Anger Hurts.
Oakland, CA. New Harbinger Pub. Inc. 2003

Malone, T. Art of Intimacy.
N.Y. Prentiss Hall Press. 1987

Menninger, W. Coping with Anxiety.
N.J. Jason Aronson, Inc.1996

Mercola, J. MD. *Effortless Healing.9 Simple Ways...*
N.Y. Harmony Books. 2015

Minirth, F. *In Pursuit of Happiness.*
Grand Rapids, MI. Baker Book House. 2004

Murphy, J. *The Power of Your Subconscious Mind*: ...
N.J. Reward Books. Revised 2000

Niven, D. 100 Simple Secrets of Happy People.
N.Y. HarperCollins Pub. 2000

Papolos, D. Overcoming Depression.
N.Y. HarperCollins Pub.1997

Potter-Efron, R.& P. Letting Go of Anger.
Oakland, CA. New Harbinger Pub. Inc.1995

Potter-Efron, R & P. Reclaim Your Relationship:
N.J. John Wiley & Sons, Inc. 2006

Rich, P. Healing Journey of Couples.
N.Y. John Wiley & Sons, Inc.1998

Richardson, C. Take Time for Your Life.
N.Y. Broadway Books. Random House. 1999

Satterfield, J.,(CDs) Cognitive Behavioral Therapy:
Techniques for Retraining Your Brain.
Chantilly, VA. The Great Courses 2015

Seligman, M. Learned Optimism.
N.Y. Pocket Books. Simon & Schuster, Inc.1990

Seligman, M. What You Can Change.
N.Y. Alfred A. Knopf. 1993

Seligman, M. Authentic Happiness.
N.Y. Free Press. Simon & Schuster, Inc. 2002

Sheikh, J. ed. Treating the Elderly.
San Francisco, CA. Jossey-Bass Pub.1996

Schiraldi, G. Self-Esteem Workbook.
Oakland, CA. New Harbinger Pub., Inc. 2001

Shimoff, M. Happy for No Reason.
N.Y. Free Press. 2008

Thase, M. Beating the Blues.
N.Y. Oxford University Press. 2004

Walsh, T. Beyond Psychology: a Spiritual Side.
Melbourne, FL. Harbour House Pub. 1990

Williams, MB. PTSD Workbook.
Oakland, CA. New Harbinger Pub., Inc. 2002